AF327109

In this print from an 1887 issue of Puck magazine, the old favorites in children's literature are upset over the new adventure and scientific books that became popular toward the end of the 19th century. Despite their plea to the young boy, progress in different directions was indeed a must. Drawn by F. Opper, lithographed by J. Ottmann. (10½″ by 14″).

Children's Books of the 19th Century

Lou W. McCulloch

Photo Illustrations by Thomas R. McCulloch

Wallace-Homestead Book Co.
1912 Grand Avenue
Des Moines, Iowa 50305

Library of Congress Catalog
Card Number 77-87948

ISBN 0-87069-239-9

Published By

Wallace-Homestead Book Co.
1912 Grand Avenue
Des Moines, Iowa 50305

Table Of Contents

Introduction

Whatever our age, there is a little bit of child in all of us. Perhaps this is the reason why collectors are attracted to children's books, for they represent an escape into other worlds and a trip back into the past. It is not surprising that so many examples of various children's publications have survived to be discovered by a caring collector today, for during the nineteenth century such literature was treasured by the recipient. It was not unusual to ascribe a particular meaning to the presenting of a book to a child, as those given by a teacher as a reward of merit. Such tokens were, of course, kept as mementos throughout a lifetime.

And unlike the extensive libraries available to children today, a child of a hundred and fifty years ago may have had only a single school book and a few editions to call his own. Country schools rarely could afford to give a textbook to each child during the school year, so geography and arithmetic books were usually shared with a number of others. Even in the private schools books were considered school property, although diligent students were required to copy extensive passages for their own use. For this reason, such examples are more likely to be found in a worn condition and represent a challenge to a collector of only prime specimens.

It is conceivable that any early children's book in "as printed" condition has value. Of course, there are some that have obtained more value than others, depending on subject matter, demand, edition, author, or illustrations. For instance, an illustrated chapbook about insects and flora would probably be more desirable to a collector than a small book of poetry without woodcuts or engravings. Likewise, a first edition is preferred over a latter printing, and many limit their collection to acquiring these "hard to find" examples.

Some prefer to obtain only books containing a certain classic tale, as "The Children in the Woods" or "Robinson Crusoe." Although such a practice may well produce one of the finest topical collections, it places limitations on the collector and decreases the chance for a discovery. After all, a true appreciation for old children's books is usually based on the excitement felt when an item from the past is found, the tactility of the aged paper, the variety of old type, the story with its connotations, and most often, the uniqueness of the illustrations.

Whatever your interest, there is more than likely a children's book that will be found appealing to you. Besides the classics and geographies, there are alphabet primers, religious and moral tales, historical narratives, mechanicals, and poetry.

Do not be discouraged in your scourings, for an old book can be found in the most unlikely of places. Although the flea markets, book auctions, antique shows, and garage sales are generally your best bet, you may find your most prized acquisition in a battered cardboard box in your attic. From personal experience the author has found that it is better to pass up examples that are torn or damaged, even though a purchase has not been made for "many a moon" and the urge for an addition to your collection is almost overwhelming. It is better to save your funds for the prime examples.

Of course, very early editions from the first part of the nineteenth century usually bear much use, just as the contemporary almanacs from this period, and thus "foxing" and edge wear are common. It is possible to find specimens that are in nearly pristine condition, because the rag content in the paper was high, making a more durable publication.

Ironically, some chapbooks and primers have survived over two hundred years, when books printed as recently as twenty years ago are showing signs of disintegration from acidity content in the paper. It would be such a waste to have a book or paper backed pamphlet survive a century and then have it destroyed by a collector who unknowingly used improper storage. Believe me, one treasure damaged by tape, glue, humidity, or bent pages is too high a price to pay.

A CHAPMAN.

From "The Cries and Habits of the City of London,' by M. Lauron, 1709.

A London chapman plies his wares in the early 18th century. Frontispiece to "Chapbooks of the Eighteenth Century," by John Ashton, London, 1882.

Chapter 1

Chapbooks and Penny Histories

"Fair Diomed, you do as Chapmen do, Dispraise the thing that you desire to buy."
Shakespeare in "Troilus and Cressida," Act iv, sc. 1.

As the quote from Shakespeare indicates, the chapmen who peddled their penny histories and wares throughout English villages were aware that excessive censure could sometimes produce a sale, an attitude akin to the psychological appeal of the chapbooks they were selling.

Whether chapbooks is a corruption of "cheap," derived from the ancient slang "ceap" meaning trade or based on the fact that "chap" men peddled such pamphlets, there is no doubt that the chapbook came to America from England. There is some confusion as to what a chapbook constitutes. Is it strictly a story for children, a religious tract, or simply any paperbound pamphlet of the 19th century? In the following text, the answers to these questions will be examined.

First, it should be made clear that chapbooks can be traced to the 16th century in England, and similar publications originated even earlier in France. Chapbooks were not printed to appeal uniquely to children for they were purchased mainly by parents, and thus printers picked titles that attracted an adult's attention, such as "Adopted" or "Bravery and Happy Death of James Covey." Morbidity was prevalent in early printings, as well as an obsession for journeys by land or sea. Undoubtedly, tales about different parts of the world were of interest because travel was limited for the majority of families.

These paperbound books that sold for pennies were affordable by the common folk and portrayed stories written at approximately their reading level. This is

[No. 89.

THE

DAIRYMAN.

BY REV. D. TYERMAN.

See page 7.

PRINTED FOR

THE AMERICAN TRACT SOCIETY.

1825.

Title page of the "Dairyman" with woodcut illustration, published by the American Tract Society, 1825. (4″ by 6½″).

THE

BOOK OF THE SEA;

FOR THE INSTRUCTION OF

LITTLE SAILORS.

NEW YORK:

KIGGINS & KELLOGG,

88 JOHN STREET.

"The Book of the Sea" offered information about sea voyages and types of ships. Published by Kiggins & Kellogg, New York, circa the 1840's. (2½" by 3½").

Title page of "The History of Goody Two Shoes" with hand-colored woodcuts, circa 1850's. (4½" by 6").

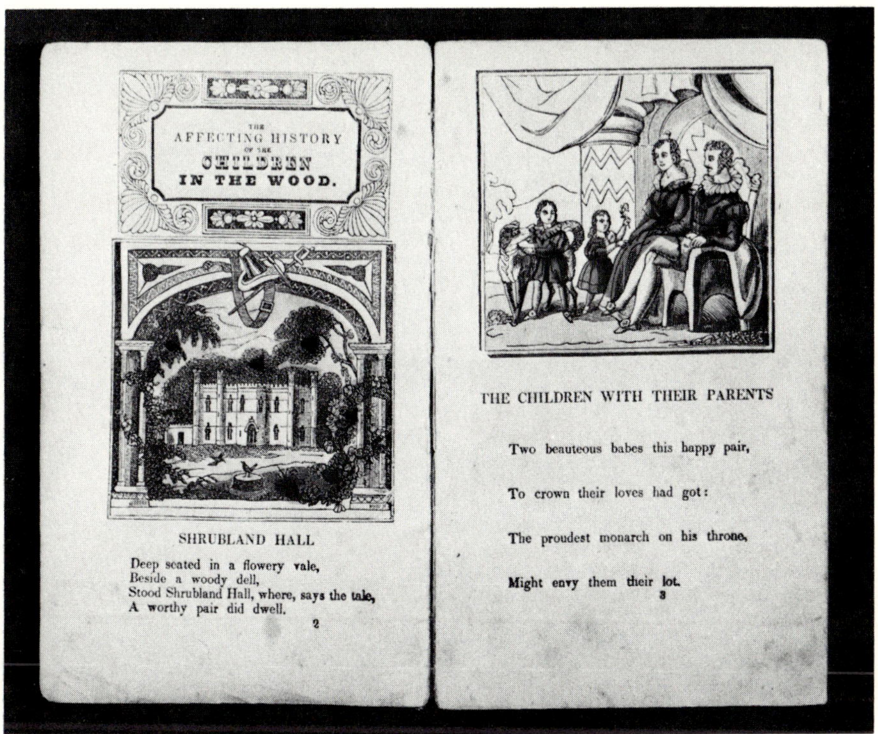
THE AFFECTING HISTORY OF THE CHILDREN IN THE WOOD.

SHRUBLAND HALL

Deep seated in a flowery vale,
Beside a woody dell,
Stood Shrubland Hall, where, says the tale,
A worthy pair did dwell.

2

THE CHILDREN WITH THEIR PARENTS

Two beauteous babes this happy pair,

To crown their loves had got:

The proudest monarch on his throne,

Might envy them their lot.

3

"The Affecting History of the Children in the Wood," was a popular chapbook that originated as a ballad. Published by J. Pease, Albany, New York, circa 1840.

not meant as a criticism, for obviously it is remarkable that in the 1700's and the first part of the 1800's many isolated families learned to read from these chapbooks, and likewise, primers.

It is a fact that chapbooks were some of the first printed matter to roll off the American presses, thus being a necessity not to be left in the English homeland. When first printed in England, they were peddled by "running stationers" in large, uncut sheets with as many as sixteen pages reproduced on a single sheet. The printer displayed such sheets on the walls of his shop or used them as a broadside to advertise. Persons entering the shop could select whatever tales they desired and then have them properly bound, either singly or several in a hard cover book. In America, chapbooks were usually bound with an outer wrapper of coarse brown paper or wallpaper added by the owner for protection from wear. The binding was stitched by hand or a strip of material was glued in place as a reinforcement.

It is true that chapbooks appealed to children, most likely because they contained some of the first attempts at illustration. Although offering only crude woodcuts, sometimes fashioned by a printer with little artistic talent, they were preferable to the somewhat boring and difficult classics that preceded them. It was also the task of the printer to edit the text and fit the wordings on a set number of pages, so often grammar and story context were disregarded. There is no doubt that these pamphlets were the comic books of their time, with easily

Two woodcuts from circa 1820's chapbooks display the artist's balanced use of darks and lights as well as decorative borders. Top: from, "Sweets for Leisure Hours." Bottom: "The Sun-Flower."

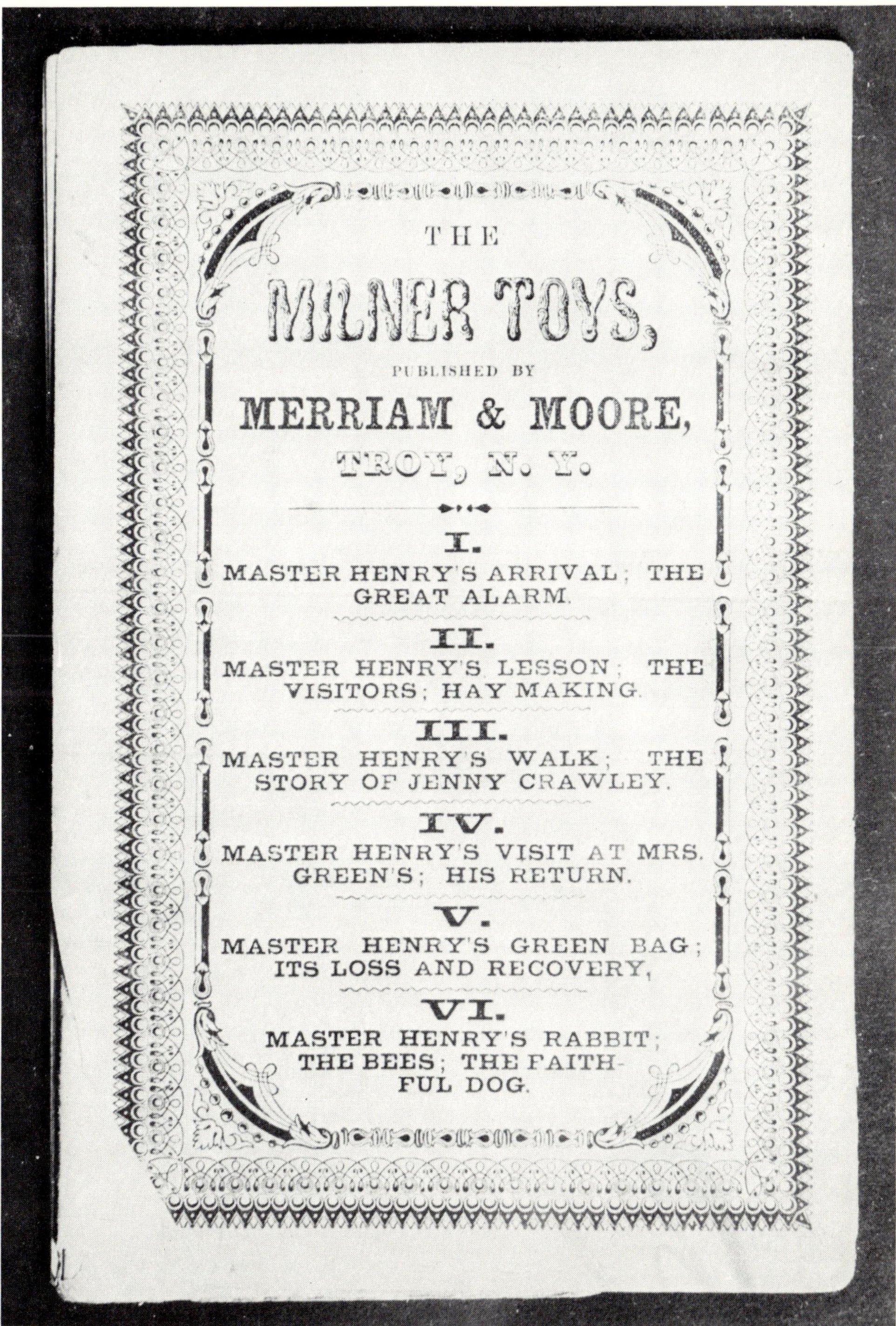
THE
MILNER TOYS,
PUBLISHED BY
MERRIAM & MOORE,
TROY, N. Y.
I.
MASTER HENRY'S ARRIVAL; THE GREAT ALARM.
II.
MASTER HENRY'S LESSON; THE VISITORS; HAY MAKING.
III.
MASTER HENRY'S WALK; THE STORY OF JENNY CRAWLEY.
IV.
MASTER HENRY'S VISIT AT MRS. GREEN'S; HIS RETURN.
V.
MASTER HENRY'S GREEN BAG; ITS LOSS AND RECOVERY,
VI.
MASTER HENRY'S RABBIT; THE BEES; THE FAITHFUL DOG.

Reverse of the chapbook, "Master Henry's Rabbit," advertising the Milner Toys. Chapbooks were synonymously known as toybooks in America. (3¾″ x 5¾″).

read text and quaint pictorial representations.

The stories, or penny histories as they were known in England, were not at first written for entertainment, and humor was almost an unheard-of ingredient. The purpose of such publications at their institution was to offer an educational guide to proper behavior and to counteract any attraction toward fictional readings. Later, the fable was introduced with the inevitable moral or maxim incorporated in the tale. There were a few humorous chapbooks that emerged in the 1820's, as one entitled "Amusing Riddles," but most parents favored a stricter attitude in their purchases and the children rarely were allowed to read such frivolous matter.

In America, chapbooks were popularly called toybooks, and differed from their English counterparts in that they did not always copy previously printed tales and tended to offer more local background. Even the name "toy" book seems to indicate that the American versions were taken more or less in a light-hearted vein.

Whereas many English stories took place in far-off countries, as India or Africa, the American chapbook locations were less complicated, as on the beach in "Harry the Shrimper" or in a garden in "The Broken Arm," both published circa 1840. A strictly American interpretation was the narratives regarding captivities, hardships, and life among the Indians. Such pamphlets were eagerly sought by New England families, longing for a "true" account of life on the plains. Surely these chapbooks were the forerunners of the modern day Western adventure tale.

After the first part of the 19th century, chapbooks became smaller in size than the 4 inch by 6 inch standard size, and thus later examples can sometimes be dated in this manner. Unfortunately, the Revolutionary War helped to bring about the demise of the chapbook, for the newspaper gained recognition during this period. The newspaper was a more timely method of teaching history and awareness and obviously a printer could gain more subscriptions from such publications. Instead, the chapbooks were labeled as children's fare and placed on the shelves with the classical series. By the middle of the century, the toybooks were as obsolete as the literary content of the tales. Although publishers, as

Top left: "Elmina," a tale for young people, listed the alphabet on the inside cover; New Haven, 1806. Top right: "The Sunflower," adapted from an English version, printed by S. Babcock, circa the 1820's. Bottom: Hard cover chapbook, "The Broken Arm," William Wood & Co., New York, circa 1830's.

The frontispiece of "Master Henry's Rabbit" displayed a Western scene, The Hunter's Life, circa 1840.

Peter Parley, the pseudonym of S.G. Goodrich, became associated with over a hundred works designed for children, from "Stories About America" to "Parley's Story of the Bird's Nest." Softbound, "Peter Parley's Story of the Little Soldiers," 1829, S.G. Goodrich & Co., Boston. (4″ x 5¼″).

McLoughlin Brothers, retained the toy-book format, the stories and illustrations had turned from the moralistic overtones to the realistic approach found in some children's literature of today.

Chapbooks were frequently reprinted by the religious tract societies, but the terms of chapbook and tract can not be used interchangeably. They were printed for different purposes, the chapbook being an educational instructor and the tract a method of instilling religious teachings. Yet, the original idea of furthering education is mentioned in a quote introducing an 1820 listing of the publications of the American Tract Society, as follows:

> "The benefits to be derived from Education may be greatly assisted by the dispersion of small cheap Tracts on religious and moral duties."
>
> —Bishop of Durham.

The education in this statement was not referring to facts of geography or history, but to enlighten a child to his sinful ways. Whereas a chapbook may have frightened a child into proper behavioral submission with crude woodcuts, such as the depiction of the death

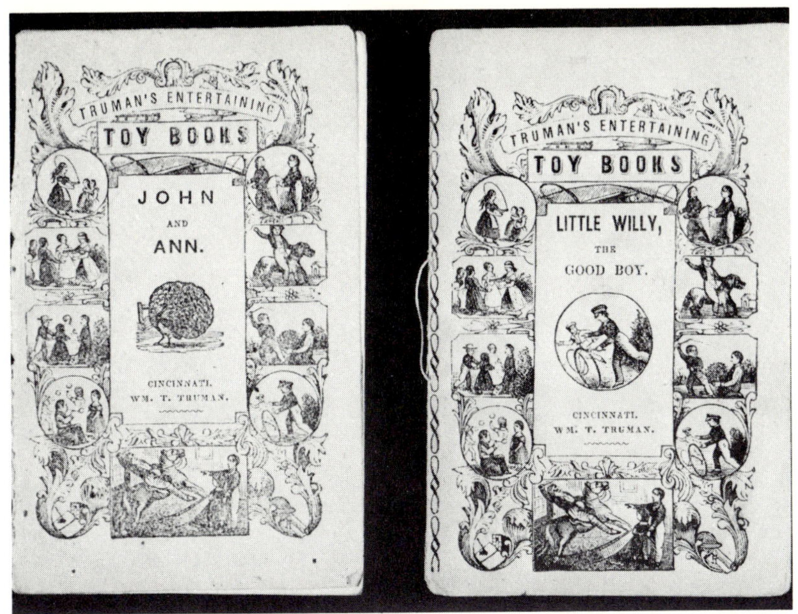

Truman's Entertaining Toy Books contained stories about playtime activities. Cincinnati, Wm. T. Truman, circa the 1840's. (Each 2¾″ by 4¼″).

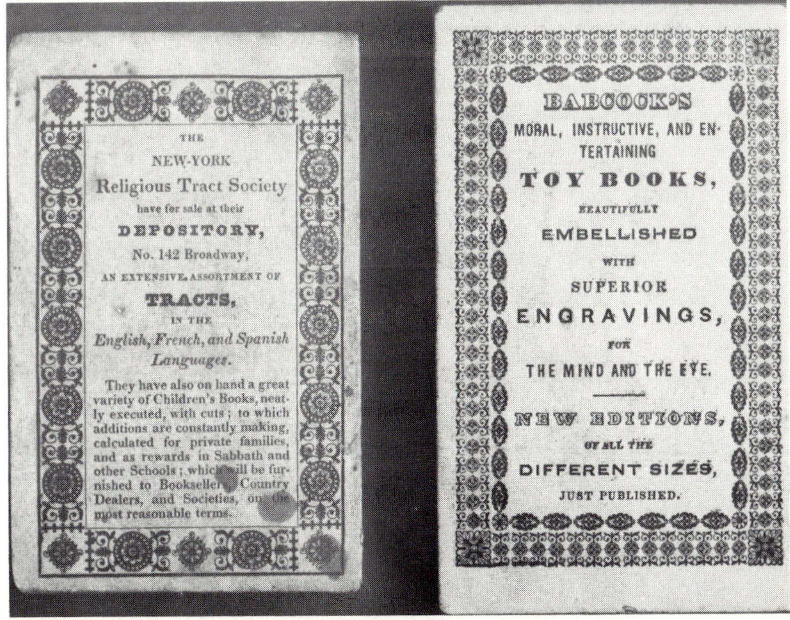
THE
NEW-YORK
Religious Tract Society
have for sale at their
DEPOSITORY,
No. 142 Broadway,
AN EXTENSIVE ASSORTMENT OF
TRACTS,
IN THE
English, French, and Spanish Languages.

They have also on hand a great variety of Children's Books, neatly executed, with cuts; to which additions are constantly making, calculated for private families, and as rewards in Sabbath and other Schools; which will be furnished to Booksellers, Country Dealers, and Societies, on the most reasonable terms.

BABCOCK'S
MORAL, INSTRUCTIVE, AND ENTERTAINING
TOY BOOKS,
BEAUTIFULLY
EMBELLISHED
WITH
SUPERIOR
ENGRAVINGS,
FOR
THE MIND AND THE EYE.

NEW EDITIONS,
OF ALL THE
DIFFERENT SIZES,
JUST PUBLISHED.

Left: An advertisement for religious tracts makes the distinction of having on hand a great variety of children's books; whereas, right: S. Babcock advertises "moral, instructive, and entertaining toybooks." Note the decorative borders, circa the 1820's.

"The Child's Gift" offered stories from "The Kitty Whiner" to "On Receiving a Flower." Printed by the American S.S. Union, Philadelphia, circa the 1820's. (3″ by 4¼″).

Belle Boyd giving tract booklets to prisoners during the Civil War.

of the "Babes in the Woods," the tract threatened with the rhetorical use of "Hell, fire and brimstone."

The chapbook evolved into entertaining children's stories and the tract became a source of religious sustenance. For this reason, the tract alone survived into the late 19th century and was used extensively as pamphlet literature, given free of charge by dedicated individuals.

Most chapbooks can be classified into one or more of the following catagories: religious instruction, supernatural interpretations, romantic legends, ballad tales, and historical narratives. Some of the first chapbooks were based on ballads, such as "The Two Children in the Wood" printed originally as a ballad in 1597 entitled, "The Norfolk Gentleman, His Will and Testament." Thus the ballad was the predecessor of the chapbook. "Goody Two-Shoes," first printed in 1786 in Worcester, Mass. by Isaiah Thomas of almanac fame, was a romantic legend of two orphans that "make it good." "Valentine and Orson" was perhaps the most well-known historical narrative that came from France about 1510. It recounted a tale of twin princes born in the inevitable woods and reared by a bear. It is interesting that psychologists today are finding out that the reoccurring dark woods in children's literature is based on an inner fear that is universal, that of overcoming adversity.

Prolific printers of the American toybooks were usually from small towns. Examples have been noted from Sidney's Press, New Haven (1806); Hazeltine & Co., Warren, Pa. (circa 1830's); McKay & Sleeper, Waterford, Pa. (1830's); E.H. Pease & Co., Albany, N.Y. (1840's); S. Babcock, New Haven (1820's), and Merriam & Moore, Troy, N.Y. (1840's). Tracts were published by the American Tract Society at their depository in New York City after its foundation in 1820.

In conclusion, a chapbook was not strictly a story for children, a religious tract or just any paperbound pamphlet. It was a forerunner to many modern literary forms including children's books, Western tales, and even the comic book.

If one is interested in acquiring these small books, examine any stack of paper memorabilia at an antique show or flea market. There were thousands of chapbooks published and there are still some waiting to be discovered by a knowing collector. If you are lucky, as I was at a show last summer, you can pick up an 1825 copy of "The Dairyman" for a mere fifty cents, but be prepared for much higher prices from those who realize the value of a penny history.

THE ROCKET.

CHAPTER I.

LIFE AMONG THE COAL-PITS.

WHAT useful little fellow is this, carrying his father's dinner to him at the coal-pit? He takes care, also, of his little brothers and

An 1860 chapbook entitled "The Rocket" discussed amusements of poor children and "life among the coal-pits." Stories as these offered children scientific information as well as facts of life.

Related Books and Current Values

"Master Henry's Rabbit," Merriam & Moore Pub., Troy, N.Y., illustrated with woodcuts, paper wraps, 4″ x 6″, Milner Toy Series, value $10.

"The Poor Old Soldier and His Dog," Marks Toy-books, published by Fisk & Little, 82 State St., Albany, N.Y., handcolored illustrations, paper wraps, 4″ x 6″, circa 1850's, value $25.

"Sports For All Seasons", T.W. Strong, 98 Nassau St., N.Y., circa 1840's, handcolored paper wraps, illustrations, 4″ x 6″, value $20.

"The Wise Boys," or the Entertaining Histories of Luke Lovebook, etc., edited by Mrs. S.J. Hale, engravings, published by Edwd. Dunigan, 151 Fulton St., N.Y., circa 1850, value $18.

"Proverbs for the Nursery," gilt covers, four color illustrations, published by McLoughlin Brothers, N.Y., circa 1860's, value $8.

"The Broken Arm," pub. by William Wood & Co., 61 Walker St., N.Y., illustrated, value $4.

"Sammy Tickletooth," Aunt Grumbles Series, McLoughlin Brothers, N.Y., illustrated, paper wraps, 4″ x 6″, value $4.

"Elmina; or the Flower that Never Fades, a Tale for Young People," Sidney's Press, New Haven, 1806, woodcuts, 2″ x 3½″, paper wraps, value $15.

"Sweets for Leisure Hours or Flowers of Instruction," printer S. Babcock, New Haven, woodcuts, 2″ x 3½″, value $18.

"The Little Market Woman," Ancient Nursery Rhymes Series, color illustrations, McLoughlin Bros., N.Y., circa 1860's, value $12.

"The Sun-flower of Poetical Blossoms" New Haven, printer S. Babcock, woodcuts, circa 1820's, 2″ x 3½″, value $18.

"Miss Helen's Adopted Daughter," published by E.T. Hazeltine, Warren, Pa., yellow paper wraps, 2½" x 3½", 1860's, ad on reverse, value $3.

"The Crooked Man & Other Stories," Aunt Mary's Little Series, McLoughlin Bros., N.Y., illustrated, 3½" x 5", late 1850's, value $4.

"Adopted," published by McKay & Sleeper, Waterford, Pa., yellow paper wraps, 2½" x 3½", value $2.

"Henry Brown," Father's Series, McLoughlin Bros., N.Y., color illustrations, circa 1870's, 4" x 5", value $3.50.

"Harry the Shrimper," published by William Wood & Co., 61 Walker St., N.Y., illustrated, circa 1860's, 3" x 5", value $3.

"The Slave's Friend," for sale at the Anti-Slavery Office, Corner of Nassau & Spruce Sts., N.Y., 1836, 2" x 3", value $20.

"Pretty Stories for Children," by Philip J. Cozans, 116 Nassau St., N.Y., hand-colored illustrations, paper wraps, illuminated edition, circa 1850's, value $15.

"Lost at Sea," published by E. T. Hazeltine, Warren, Pa., yellow paper wraps, 2½" x 3½", circa 1860's, value $3.

"George Mills, or The Little Boy Who Did Not Love His Books," by a Teacher, Munroe and Foster, Boston, 128 Washington St., circa 1836, 4" x 6", paper covered boards, value $4.

"Diamonds and Toads," Little Folks Series, McLoughlin Bros., N.Y., six color illustrations, circa 1860's, value $8.

"History of Master Henry," by Mrs. Sherwood, Boston, Dayton & Wentworth, 86 Washington St., 1855, woodcuts, blue hardcover, 4" x 6", value $6.

"Santa Claus and His Works," Big Picture Series, McLoughlin Bros., N.Y., six color illustrations, circa 1860's, value $18.

"The Robin's Christmas Eve," Uncle Ned's Picture Books Series, McLoughlin Bros., N.Y., circa 1860's, four color illus., value $10.

"Fanny Overkind," J. Wrigley Publisher, 61 Chatham St., N.Y. 4" x 6", hand-colored cover, circa 1850's, value $20.

"Story of the Little Drummer," from the Pretty Primer, Huestis & Cozans, 104 Nassau St., N.Y., circa 1820's, 4″ x 6″, value $10.

"Lily's Picture Book," McLoughlin Bros., N.Y., gilt covers, circa 1870, four color illustrations, 6″ x 9″, value $4.50.

"Happy Changes With the Lives of Charles Candid and Peter Polish," edited by Mrs. S. J. Hale, published by Edw. Dunigan, 151 Fulton St., N.Y., eight stereotyped engravings, circa 1850, value $8.

"The Little Frankie Series" (six volumes), by Mrs. Madeline Leslie, Boston, Crosby and Nichols, 117 Washington St., 5″ x 6″, green hardcover, value $20 for set.

"Little Dame Crump" Mark's Toy Books, published by Fisk & Little, 82 State St., Albany, N.Y., paper wraps, hand-colored illustrations, 4″ x 6″, circa 1850, value $20.

"Mrs Elliot's Stories: The Bird Nest," McLoughlin Bros., 24 Beekman St., N.Y., paper wraps, hand-colored illustrations, circa 1850's, value $15.

Virtuous and moral attitudes were constant ingredients in 19th century children's literature and its illustration. From "Conscience" by Mrs. Follen, Boston, 1873. (4½" by 6").

Chapter 2

Of Morals and Religion

"How shall the young secure their hearts,
And guard their lives from sin?
Thy word the choicest rules imparts,
To keep the conscience clean."
—Advice from a Master to His Apprentice,
by the American Tract Society, 1825.

A clean conscience was, indeed, one of the prerequisites for survival in the nineteenth century. A strident religious attitude permeated every corner of children's literature, from the simple primer to the obviously church-oriented Bible stories. In fact, the churches and related tract societies contributed a major part to the development of such literature.

It was a miniature Bible that instigated a possible interest in creating reading matter for children. During the 17th century in England, it was a novelty to print the Bible and other religious oriented volumes in miniature form. Thus, a gentleman traveling could easily carry along a whole library of books if he so desired. What was not expected by the printers, was that these minuscule volumes were overwhelmingly attractive to children and achieved the affectionate title of "thumb" Bibles.

John Weever's book of 1601, "An Agnus Dei," was one of the models for these volumes. The simple text and rhyming phrases became a format adaptable to all forms of children's literature, from an alphabet book to the New England Primer. Of course, at that time the religious publications were considered the only proper reading matter for children. Any other books might contain sinful influence or expose a child to the evil ways of the world.

Other types of books that were unexpectedly attractive to children were the

There are the Bears tearing the children. Oh what
icked children they were! See page 94.

THE

CHILD'S BIBLE.

WITH PLATES.

By a Lady of Cincinnati.

FISHER & BROTHER,

PHILADELPHIA, NEW YORK, BALTIMORE, AND BOSTON

Miniature books with plates were a novelty. "The Child's Bible" of 1834 was written "by a Lady of Cincinnati" and printed by Fisher & Brother. It measures 2″ by 2¼."

in the judgment of the papists, heretics; and they were condemned to be burnt.

The day being come when these innocents should suffer, July 18, 1556, in the place where they stood to con-

The Rev. John Fox's "Book of Martyrs" was perused by children with a sense of fear. The portrayal of "triumphant deaths" and various massacres unfortunately became the prototype for many moralistic tales to follow. From an 1851 illustrated edition, Boston.

"The Permission" as seen in "The Child's Book of Bible Stories" was part of a series of illustrations regarding the fall of man. By Rev. T. H. Gallaudet, American Tract Society, New York, circa the 1830's.

religious editions with pictorial representations of tortured individuals, such as "Foxe's Book of Martyrs," published in London in 1562. Similar illustrations of martyrs being burned at the stake were retained in children's primers even through the mid-19th century. The New England Primer of 1850 still brandished a woodcut on the paper cover of the burning of John Rogers, the first martyr in Queen Mary's reign. The text refering to this terrifying illustration noted that he, ". . . with wonderful patience, died courageously for the gospel of Jesus Christ."

This attraction by children to morbid and horrific tales was perhaps caused by the death, sickness, and destruction that surrounded a typical child's life. The child who lived near the coastal regions heard daily of ship disasters, whereas every child in the country areas knew the dangers of the elements and the fear of sickness in a family. Unfortunately, these fears were capitalized on by the churches and used as tools to instill "wisdom" and proper behavior. Joyful deaths, particularly of children, were found in many tract stories and can be traced to James Janeway's accounts of conversions and subsequent happy deaths mentioned in his Token Series, printed in London in the latter 1670's and reprinted up until the 1830's.

In a typical behavioral-slanted publication from the 1850's, the American Baptist Society offered pictures entitled, "Kindness Rewarded", "The Sunday-School Scholar", "Mind Your Mother", and "The Useful Boy." The text under "Mind Your Mother" stated, "See that poor prisoner! Once he was a happy, playful child like you; now he is a wicked murderer. He did not mind his mother . . . he went with bad boys who taught him bad habits . . . until one day, when

NO. 125.

FATAL EFFECTS OF Ardent Spirits.

BY REV. EBENEZER PORTER, D. D.

In the winter of 1805, a stranger perished in the snow, with a bottle of spirits at his side, in the town where the author then resided. The following pages were occasioned by that event.

PUBLISHED BY THE

AMERICAN TRACT SOCIETY,

AND SOLD AT THEIR DEPOSITORY, NO. 144 NASSAU-STREET, NEAR THE CITY-HALL, NEW-YORK; AND BY AGENTS OF THE SOCIETY, ITS BRANCHES, AND AUXILIARIES, IN THE PRINCIPAL CITIES AND TOWNS IN THE UNITED STATES.

Vol. 4. Q

The portraying of man's vices was supposed to frighten a child into obedience. From the American Tract Society, 1825.

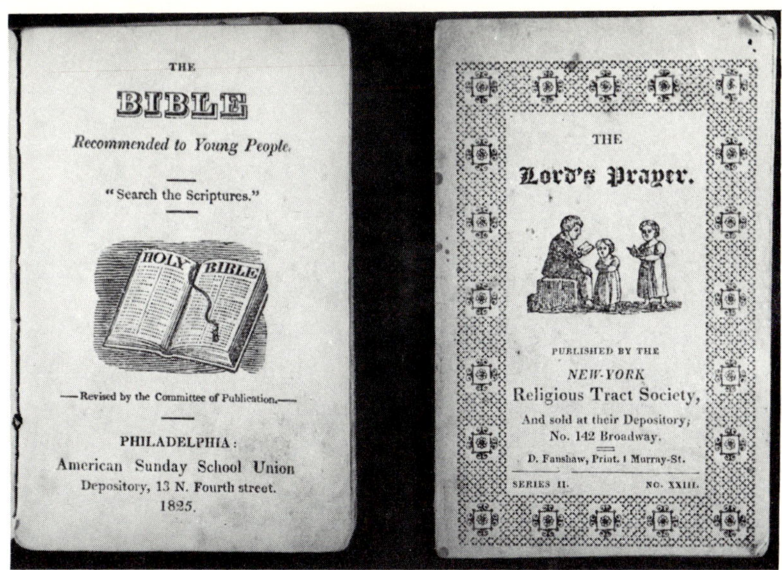
THE

BIBLE

Recommended to Young People.

"Search the Scriptures."

HOLY BIBLE

—Revised by the Committee of Publication.—

PHILADELPHIA:

American Sunday School Union

Depository, 13 N. Fourth street.

1825.

THE

Lord's Prayer.

PUBLISHED BY THE

NEW-YORK

Religious Tract Society,

And sold at their Depository;

No. 142 Broadway.

D. Fanshaw, Print. 1 Murray-St.

SERIES II. NO. XXIII.

Left: The New York Religious Tract Society warned children in their interpretation of the Lord's Prayer that, "you are not too young to die." D. Fanshaw printer, circa 1820, (2½″ by 4¼″). Right: This Bible by the American Sunday School Union was "revised by the Committee of Publication." Printed at Philadelphia, 1825. (2½″ by 4″).

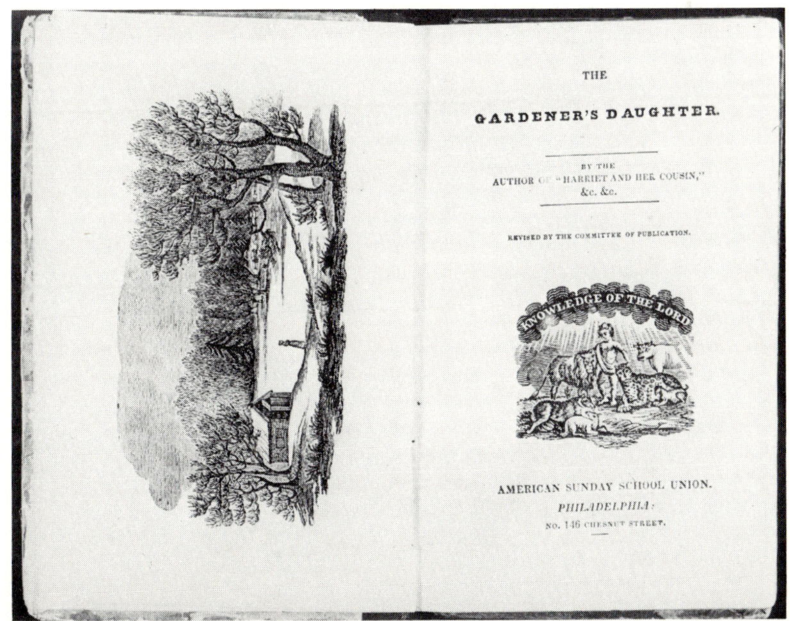
THE

GARDENER'S DAUGHTER.

BY THE

AUTHOR OF "HARRIET AND HER COUSIN,"

&c. &c.

REVISED BY THE COMMITTEE OF PUBLICATION.

KNOWLEDGE OF THE LORD

AMERICAN SUNDAY SCHOOL UNION.

PHILADELPHIA:

NO. 146 CHESNUT STREET.

It was common to incorporate religious teachings within the framework of a story about everyday life. From "The Gardener's Daughter," American Sunday School Union, Philadelphia, circa 1830's. (7″ by 5½″).

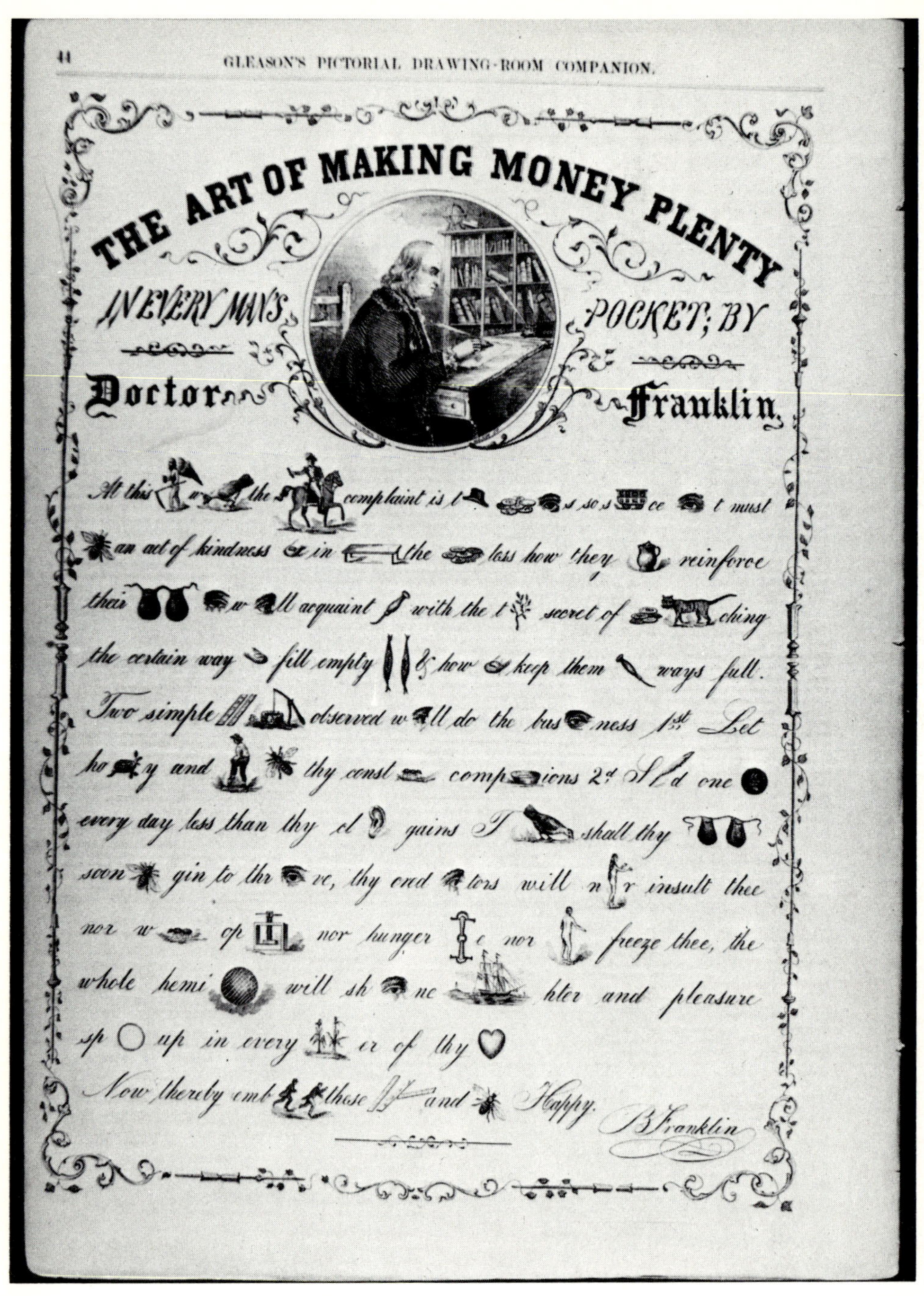
44 GLEASON'S PICTORIAL DRAWING-ROOM COMPANION.

THE ART OF MAKING MONEY PLENTY

IN EVERY MAN'S POCKET; BY

Doctor Franklin.

At this the complaint is t s so s ce t must
an act of kindness & in the less how they reinforce
their w ll acquaint with the t secret of ching
the certain way fill empty & how keep them ways full.
Two simple observed w ll do the bus ness 1st Let
ho y and thy const comp ions 2d S d one
every day less than thy cl gains T shall thy
soon gin to thr ve, thy cred tors will n r insult thee
nor w op nor hunger e nor freeze thee, the
whole hemi will sh ne lter and pleasure
sp up in every er of thy
Now thereby emb these and Happy.
B Franklin

An 1854 copy of Benjamin Franklin's famous hieroglyphic interpretation of "The Art of Making Money Plenty." This emblematic technique was applied to children's story books and also to rebus puzzles.

drunk, he killed a man." The portraying of man's vices was another method of frightening the young, showing the adverse effects of the "poison" and various other unhealthy amusements. In short, a child was expected to become knowledgeable to the ways of the adult world before he was permitted to be a child.

A child's Bible printed in 1827 in Philadelphia offered directions for interpretation of the scriptures. The narrow-mindedness of these small, paper-wrapped books is exemplified by a statement to the young by an ominous Dr. Young. He relates, "You may with propriety desire to know some things which is not the business of the Bible to teach, but these are of very little importance, compared with what it does teach." Even as early as 1759, a London edition of the "Children's Bible" carried the declaration that, "The Bible is no fit plaything for children."

Whether Bible quotations or stories should be presented in an entertaining manner was apparently a problem. The solution seems to have been found in the use of illustrations, for a picture was found to hold a child's attention considerably longer than any religious text.

The Emblem Books, created in 1531 by a Milanese, solved this dilemma by combining the religious lessons with symbolic woodcuts or engravings. Emblematical figures ranged from creatures of nature to those of a moralistic tone, as the "Disobedient Child." Even John Bunyan wrote a book for use by children entitled, "Divine Emblems: or Temporal Things Spiritualized," printed in London about 1790. This use of symbolic pictures, sometimes completely unrelated to the context of a story, was to predominate children's literature throughout the first half of the 19th century.

An unusual use of emblems was applied to a book known as, "A Curious Hieroglyphic Bible," printed by Isaiah Thomas in Worcester, Mass. in 1788. Thomas, who also kept busy by producing a multitude of almanacs and chapbooks, substituted pictures of objects for certain scripture words. The whole sentences, giving explanations of the figures, were given at the bottom of each page. Undoubtedly, Thomas had seen one of T. Hodgson's editions of a hieroglyphic Bible, originally published in London in 1783. The small Hodgson book was distinguished by a frontispiece engraved on wood by Thomas Bewick and was bound in pictorial covered boards.

Isaiah Thomas was the first printer in America to use this technique for the amusement of youth and certainly instigated the use of rebuses that became a popular pastime in the latter 1880's.

Interestingly, primers also owe their origination to the Bible. As previously discussed, the Bible was considered the only proper reading matter for young people, and consequently all early books for children contained some elements of religious instruction. The first primers were books of private devotions and can be traced back to England in the 14th century. In the "Book of Hours," some English translations of Latin were offered in order that it could be used for instruction. Two hundred years later, alphabets and vowel sounds were added in order that the primers could be used as a reading guide as well as for religious sustenance. Since books specifically for reading instruction were virtually nonexistent, most early chapbooks and primers contained an alphabet on the first few pages.

The change-over from a devotional manual to a secular reading book was very gradual for the primer. Nowhere is this more evident than in the history of the printing of the "New England Primer." First published about 1686 by Benjamin Harris, this unobtrusive volume was to become one of the most widely read books, second in importance only to the Bible.

Harris had arrived in Boston after leaving London with firm political and anti-Catholic views. He had published many of his attitudes in books and broadsides previously printed in England, such as "The Protestant Tutor" and his "Protestant Petition." Certain woodcuts and rhymes from such publications were incorporated into his "New England Primer." The primer was an immediate success and printers who envied its popularity began to publish similar titles as "The Columbian Primer," "The American Primer," "The Royal Primer," and "The New York Primer." The only competitor that gained in favor was "The Royal Primer," a small book printed by John Newbery in London in the mid-1700's and later reprinted in America. This primer emulated a somewhat softer approach to religious instruction and gradually showed an influence on the noticeably harsh attitude of "The New England Primer."

The format of "The New England Primer" was to set forth an alphabet,

NO. 127.

THE

TWO SISTERS.

BY MRS. SHERWOOD,

AUTHOR OF "LITTLE HENRY AND HIS BEARER," &c. &c.

PUBLISHED BY THE

AMERICAN TRACT SOCIETY,

AND SOLD AT THEIR DEPOSITORY, NO. 144 NASSAU-STREET, NEAR THE CITY-HALL, NEW-YORK; AND BY AGENTS OF THE SOCIETY, ITS BRANCHES, AND AUXILIARIES, IN THE PRINCIPAL CITIES AND TOWNS IN THE UNITED STATES.

The story of "The Two Sisters" contained religious overtones and warned of the dangers of "vilest lusts." By Mrs. Sherwood, American Tract Society, circa 1820. 4″ by 7″.

vowel sounds and more important, moral and religious verses which were changed in almost every yearly edition. Perhaps the picture alphabet, containing twenty-four tiny woodcuts, is the portion of the book that showed the greatest influence on children's literature. The accompanying rhymes changed according to political, religious or secular sentiments that were voiced at that time. For instance, "King Charles the Good, no man of blood," became, "Kings should be good, no men of blood" and later showed disfavor by evolving to, "The British King, Lost states thirteen." Such short, rhyming verses were committed to memory by children and it was not unusual for the various churches or schools to hold contests in which each child's talents at retention were displayed. The rote method of study is still in use today.

Other indispensable ingredients of "The New England Primer" included several prayers, the Apostles Creed, Dr. Watt's Cradle Hymn, a few pages of "Instructive Questions and Answers," and most importantly, the "Westminster Assembly's Shorter Catechism." This catechism, originally composed in 1643, was urged by Cotton Mather to be copied by students and taught by parents. A second catechism was included in some primers and entitled, "Spiritual Milk for American Babes." Obviously, the "New England Primer" became a tool used to control the minds of the young and a method of testing various modes of study and dogma.

The religious tract societies took over where the "New England Primer" left off. It must be remembered that the mortality rate among children was extremely high and these societies designated themselves as the saviors of the youth. They assumed that by mass exposure to religious truths and moralistic stories, the children would be prepared for any adversity. Also, there seems to have been an outpouring of bawdy ballads and sinful literature that proliferated the streets and hawkers pack at the turn of the 19th century. The tracts, which were dispersed worldwide, were a counteractive attempt to change the tide.

The well-meaning authors of such narratives were mainly women or men who professed the title of "Reverend." Founded in 1799, the Religious Tract Society of London instigated such literature as a means of teaching religion to the masses by presenting, supposedly, nonfiction accounts of conversions. In the United States, the leading publisher of such narratives was the American

NO. 107.

LITTLE HENRY

AND

His Bearer.

BY MRS. SHERWOOD.

When he was only ten months old, he used to put his arms round his neck, and kiss him.—*See page* 3.

PUBLISHED BY THE

AMERICAN TRACT SOCIETY,

AND SOLD AT THEIR DEPOSITORY, NO. 144 NASSAU-STREET, NEAR THE CITY-HALL, NEW-YORK; AND BY AGENTS OF THE SOCIETY, ITS BRANCHES, AND AUXILIARIES, IN THE PRINCIPAL CITIES AND TOWNS IN THE UNITED STATES

Mrs. Sherwood's most popular story was an account of "Little Henry and His Bearer." It was based, in part, on her son's life. American Tract Society, circa 1820. 4″ by 7″.

Characters with names as "Mathew Merrythought" or "Luke Lovebook" were supposed to invoke an immediate image to a child. Notice the schoolroom furnishings. From "The Wise Boys" by Mrs. S.J. Hale, New York, circa the 1840's. (4¼″ by 5½″).

The Riverdale Books was just one of the series produced by Oliver Optic, the pseudonym of William T. Adams, Boston, 1871. (4½″ by 6″).

Lack of manners was often grossly exaggerated in chapbooks as "The Dirty Child" who was forsaken for a clean sister and "Sammy Tickletooth" who greedily swallowed some rising bread dough. McLoughlin Bros., late 19th century.

Tract Society, formed in 1825 by combining the New York Religious Tract Society and the New England Tract Society.

We can look back on these small volumes and chapbooks today with amusement and curiousity in regard to their meanings, but at the time of their printing, they were taken quite seriously and as truths. The tracts were delivered from house-to-house and printed in several languages as French, German, Russian, Indian, and Swedish. Brave individuals even boarded ships to distribute the truths to seamen and in a typical year dispersed eleven hundred tracts in such a manner. Not surprisingly, few were refused and according to a contemporary account, ". . . the captains and officers bore testimony to the benefits and advantages they had seen result from perusal of tracts during former voyages." Of interest to the collector are the narratives regarding temperance, as the "Fatal Effects of Ardent Spirits," classic tracts as Mrs. Sherwood's "The Two Sisters," and historical accounts as, "The Loss of the Kent."

Evidently, the outpouring of cheap repository tracts caused its own counteractive movement in the behavioral tales that followed. These "tongue in cheek" publications turned from nonfiction to the idealistic, with heroes as Luke Lovebook or Charles Candid. Subjects ranged from, "The Honours of the Table, or Rules for Behavior During Meals," printed in 1791, to an 1850 version of "Sketches of Little Girls: The Good Natured Little Girl." The sketches included chapters on the thoughtless, the vain, the forward, the slovenly, the orderly, and the snappish little girl.

Fortunately, children rather than adults, realized that such stories should not be taken seriously and that a happy medium had to be achieved between the goody-goody books and the harsh, religious attitudes exemplified in the "New England Primer" and the Sunday School tracts.

THE DRUMMER BOY.

A True Story in the American War.

LOIZEAUX BROTHERS, BIBLE TRUTH DEPOT,

63 Fourth Avenue, New York.

20 cts. per dozen; $1.25 per 100, post-paid.

True stories stemming from the Civil War appealed to boys. Softbound cover to "Charlie Coulson—The Drummer Boy," Bible Truth Depot, New York, circa the late 1860's. (3¼″ by 4¼″).

"Application" and "Idleness" were typical allegorical titles for woodcuts from moral tales, as these illustrations from a circa 1840's volume of "History of Master Henry" by Mrs. Sherwood.

"Watt's Songs of Early Religion" encompassed divine and moral verses and also favorites as the "Cradle Hymn." McLoughlin Bros., New York, circa 1870's. (3¾" by 5½").

Related Books and Current Values

"Mark Steadman; or Show Your Colors," Life Illustrated Series, originally from London Tract Society, published by American Tract Society, 150 Nassau St., N.Y., circa 1860, illustrated, hardback, 4″ x 6″, value $3.

"The Boy Makes the Man," published by T. Nelson and Sons; London, Edinburgh and N.Y., 1873, full color frontispiece and title page, illustrated, 5″ x 6″, gilted green hardback, value $7.50.

"Teacher's Tokens," six-volume set, published by Thompson, Bigelow & Brown, 29 Cornhill, Boston, 1857, illustrated red hardback, 2½″ x 3½″, value $15 for set.

"The Bible Recommended to Young People," American Sunday School Union, 148 Chestnut St., Phila., 1827, stereotyped by L. Johnson, illustrated paper wraps, 2″ x 3½″, value, $8.

"Mary Jones, or The Soldier's Daughter," American Tract Society, 150 Nassau St., N.Y., illustrated, 2½″ x 3½″, circa 1850s, value $2.50.

"Gift for Mourners, Cecil and Flavel's," by Rev. Richard Cecil, American Tract Society, 150 Nassau St., N.Y., circa 1840's, gold embossed cover, 3″ x 5″, value $10.

"The History of John Robins, the Sailor," American Sunday School Union, 148 Chestnut St., Phila., 1827, paper wraps, 2″ x 3½″, value $8.

"Under the Oak-Tree," American Tract Society, illustrated with cuts of animals and insects, paper wraps, circa 1850's, 2½″, x 3½″, value $4.50.

"The Lord's Prayer," New York Religious Tract Society, 142 Broadway, D. Fanshaw printer, woodcuts, illustrated paper wraps, circa 1810's, 2″ x 3½″, value $10.

"Milk for Babes or a Catechism in Verse," for the use of Sunday Schools, American Sunday School Union, 148 Chestnut St., Phila., 1827, paper wraps, 2″ x 3½″, value, $12.

"The Two Lambs," an allegorical history, American Sunday School Union, 148 Chestnut St., Phila., 1827, illustrated paper wraps, 2″ x 3½″, value $8.

"Evening Hours," Vol. I and II, six numbers form a volume, evangelical history, published by Munroe and Francis, by a Teacher, 128 Washington St., 1837, paper covered boards, 4″ x 6″, value $6 each volume.

"Pictures for All," American Baptist Pub. Society, 530 Arch St., Phila., circa 1860's, lith, colored wraps, 3″ x 5″, illustrated, value $4.

"Watt's Songs of Early Religion," McLoughlin Bros., N.Y., colored wraps and illustrations, 3″ x 5″, circa 1870, value $3.50.

"The Dairyman," by Rev. D. Tyerman, American Tract Society, 150 Nassau St., N.Y., woodcut on front of paper wrap, circa 1840, 4″ x 6″, value $5.

"The New England Primer," Hogan & Thompson, 30 North Fourth St., Phila., circa 1850, illustrated paper wraps plus woodcuts, 3½″ x 5″, value $8.

"Life and Death of Lady Jane Grey," American Sunday School Union, 148 Chestnut St., Phila., 1827, illustrations, paper wraps, 2″ x 3½″, value $4.

"Hymns for Children," by a Teacher, published by Munroe and Francis, 128 Washington St., 1837, paper covered boards, 4″ x 6″, value $4.

"Religion Without Learning; or the History of Susan Ward," published by American Tract Society, 144 Nassau St., N.Y., 1825, illustrated paper wraps, 4″ x 6″, value $5.50.

"The Young Cottager," #79, by Rev. Legh. Richmond, published by American Tract Society, 150 Nassau St., N.Y., circa 1860's, illustrated paper wraps, 4″ x 6″, value $3.

"Scripture Lessons for the Little Ones," American Baptist Publishing Society, 530 Arch St., Phila., circa 1860's, lith. colored wraps and illustrations, 3″ x 5″, value $4.

"The Letter Writer," by Rev. Thomas Cook, A.B., published by Charles Wells, N.Y., 1836, illustrated paper covered boards, 3½" x 5", value $6.

"Little Henry and his Bearer," by Mrs. Sherwood, American Tract Society, 144 Nassau St., N.Y., illustrated paper wraps, 1825, 4" x 6", value $10.

"The Loss of the Kent," J. Collord Printer, published by T. Mason & G. Lane, for the Union of the Methodist Episcopal Church, 200 Mulberry St., N.Y., 1838, marbled covered boards, woodcuts, 4" x 6", value $10.

"Interesting History of Mrs. Tooly, an Eminent Christian Lady in London," published by American Tract Society, 144 Nassau St., N.Y., illustrated paper wraps, 1825, 4" x 6", value $10.

"Aunt Charlotte's Stories of Bible History for the little Ones," by Charlotte M. Yonge, London and Belfast, Marcus Ward & Co., 1875, title page and frontispiece in color, value $8.

"Good Children of the Bible," Half-Hours with the Bible Series, McLoughlin Bros., N.Y., illustrated by H.W. Herrick, circa 1860's, colored paper wraps, value $4.50.

"Early Dead," published by Methodist Episcopal Sunday School Union, 200 Mulberry St., N.Y., three volumes, circa 1850's, illustrations, value $10.

"A Parting Address to a Sabbath School Child," American Tract Society, 144 Nassau St., N.Y., woodcut illustration on cover of paper wrap, 1825, 4" x 6", value $8.

"The Gardener's Daughter," by the author of "Harriet and Her Cousin," American Sunday School Union, No. 146 Chestnut St., Philadelphia, eng. frontispiece, paperboards, circa 1830's, value $5.

Chapter 3

Learning Lessons

". . . Of all reading, there is none that so readily attracts the attention, and lays hold of the sympathy of children and youth, as lively narratives of the enterprises, adventures, dangers, trials, successes, and failures of mankind."
—From Parley's first Book of History; Boston, 1859.

Reading, writing and arithmetic have been either enjoyed or despised by children for centuries, depending for the most part, on how the material was presented. Certainly a lively narrative helped to bring alive an often told event from history, such as Columbus discovering America. An engraving or woodcut picturing his landing gave an impetus to the narrative. But this was just one technique used in teaching children facts, and even though the great teachers as Peter Parley followed this method, the field was open for many authors of instruction to try out their individual ideas. And, needless to say, the competition was keen.

Besides the reliable slate and hornbook that kept the basic alphabet and rudiments of language handy for the late 18th century child, each was instructed from a few select volumes about spelling, sentence structure, history, science, and zoology. Although these categories were mainly discussed by the teacher at the local school, a curious type of book offering facts about a variety of subjects seems to have originated for the use of families in their homes. By the early 1800's, books of simple facts were included in almost every toybook publishers' line and the history book printers were obviously being influenced by the popularity of the question-and-answer format adopted in most of the small volumes.

THE

FLOCK OF SHEEP;

OR

FAMILIAR EXPLANATIONS

OF

SIMPLE FACTS.

NEW HAVEN,

PRINTED AND PUBLISHED

BY S. BABCOCK.

1840.

"The Flock of Sheep; or Familiar Explanations of Simple Facts," was printed for home use and contained a question-and-answer format. New Haven, S. Babcock, 1840. (2¾″ by 4½″).

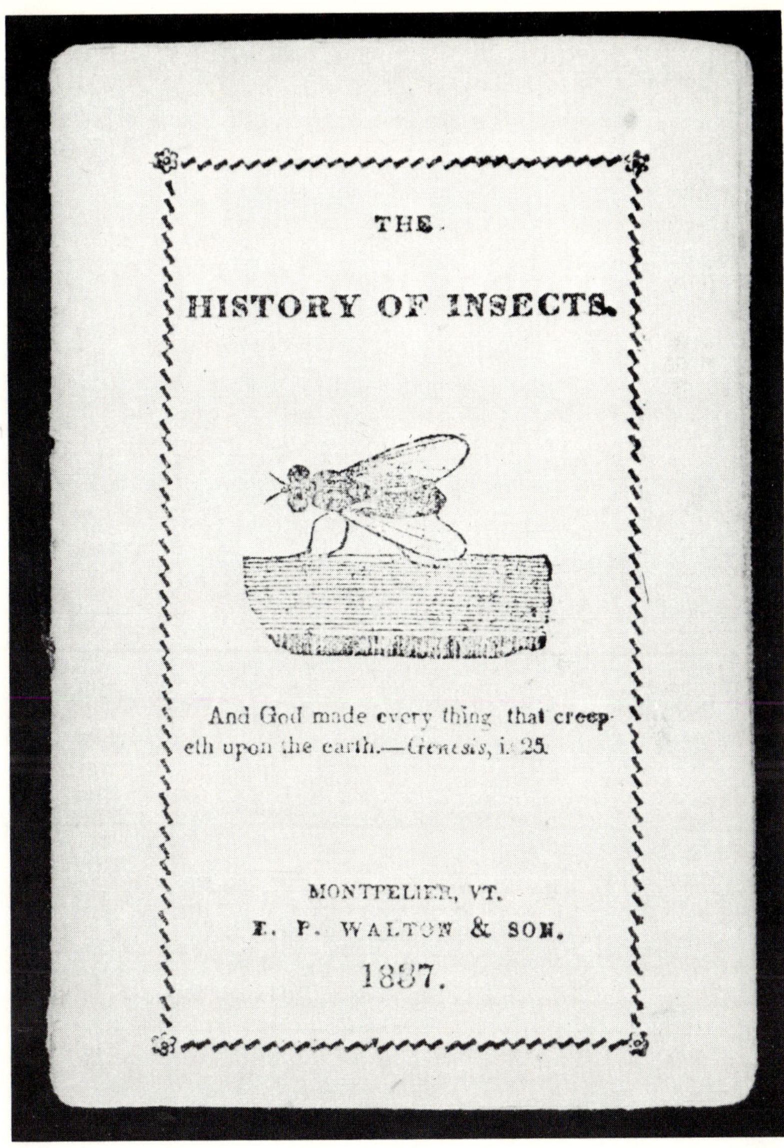

"The History of Insects," a small chapbook of 1837, contained information and plates regarding seven insects as well as an alphabet. Printed by E.P. Walton & Son of Montpelier, Vermont. (2¼″ by 3½″).

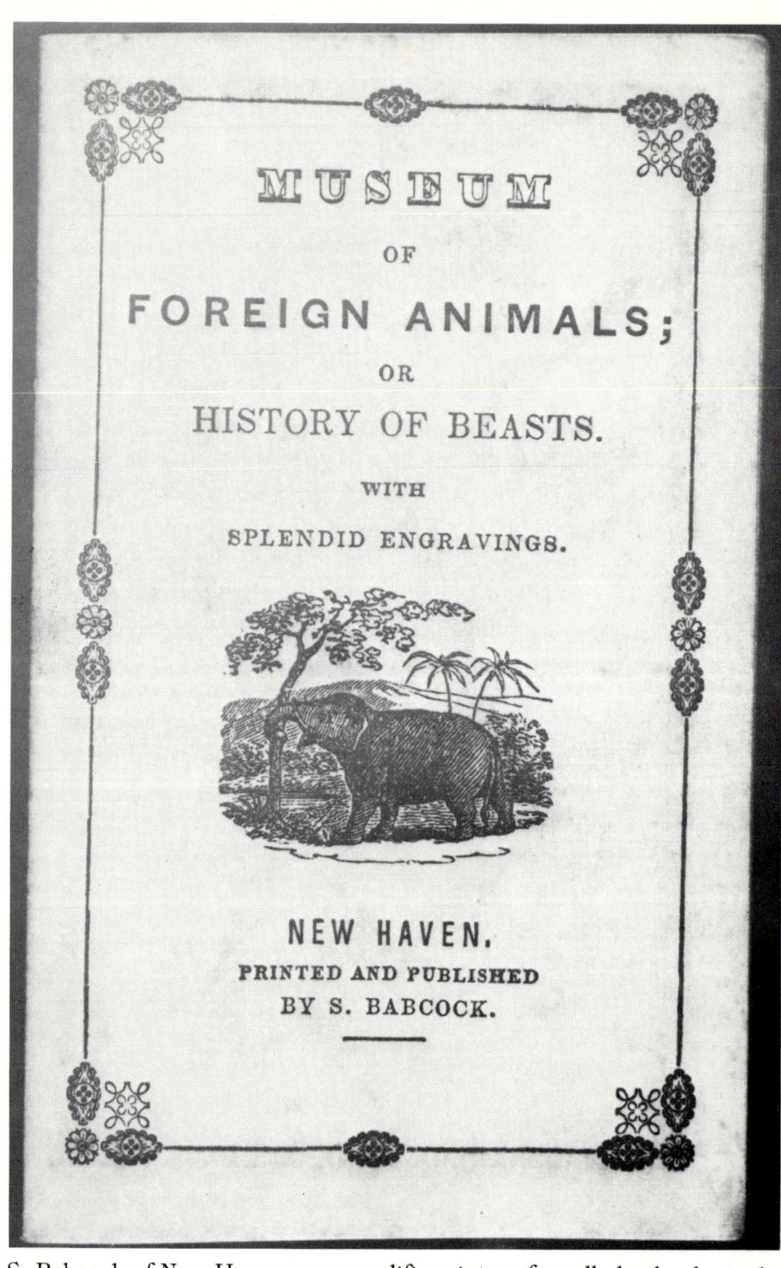

MUSEUM

OF

FOREIGN ANIMALS;

OR

HISTORY OF BEASTS.

WITH

SPLENDID ENGRAVINGS.

NEW HAVEN.

PRINTED AND PUBLISHED

BY S. BABCOCK.

S. Babcock of New Haven was a prolific printer of small chapbooks in the first half of the 19th century. The "Museum of Foreign Animals; or History of Beasts" contained engravings and descriptive text regarding animals that most American children had never seen.

For instance, in 1837 an anonymous teacher wrote of, "Conversations on Common Things" for the use of schools and families. The pictorial paper-board book, of only chapbook size, contained conversations between a mother and daughter discussing hundreds of topics, from growing an Acacia tree to manufacturing zinc. A printed dedication in the front of the volume noted that the purpose of the book was, " . . . of informing your minds and exciting you to seek after that knowledge which will be useful to you through life." S. Babcock, the prolific printer from New Haven, printed "The Flock of Sheep; or Familiar Explanations of Simple Facts" in 1840. The 2-by-3½ inch toybook with yellow paper covers featured woodcuts to illustrate each occupation or product discussed. These tiny books are filled with a myriad of unusual information and give an idea as to what life consisted of in pre-1850 days.

Children have always been fascinated by the workings of nature and the diversity of the animal kingdom and, of course, it was only natural that books on these subjects would flourish. Natural history was even incorporated into Bible stories, as in the 1852 London version, "Bible Natural History: Containing a Description of Quadrupeds, Birds, Trees, Plants, Insects, etc, mentioned in the Holy Scriptures." The conversational approach was again applied by Charles C. Reiche in 1791 when the Philadelphia edition offered, "Fifteen Discourses on the Marvelous Works in Nature, Delivered by a Father to His Children."

Although some of the depictions of animals are obviously misrepresented in the illustrations of such books, they held a certain fascination for children who had never seen such strange creatures and instilled a longing to travel to the faraway lands where the animals resided.

In another one of Babcock's toybooks of the 1840's, he mentions in his "Museum of Animals" that the . . . . "Giraffe has never been brought to this country" and is often called, "the Camelopard." Thus, the accompanying woodcut looks like a leopard spotted camel, and certainly would attract a child's attention, even today!

Flora, birds, and insects comprised another popular field of study adapted to children's literature. Thomas Bewick, the master of the woodcut, perhaps instigated an interest in portraying natural

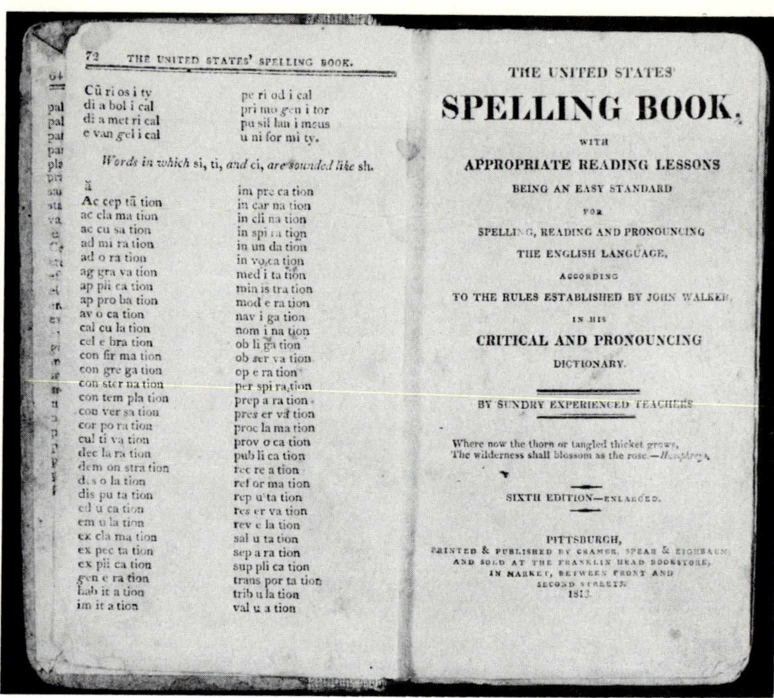

72 THE UNITED STATES' SPELLING BOOK.

Cû ri os i ty	pe ri od i cal
di a bol i cal	pri mo gen i tor
di a met ri cal	pu sil lan i mous
e van gel i cal	u ni for mi ty.

Words in which si, ti, *and* ci, *are sounded like* sh.

Ac cep tā tion	im pre ca tion
ac cla ma tion	in car na tion
ac cu sa tion	in cli na tion
ad mi ra tion	in spi ra tion
ad o ra tion	in un da tion
ag gra va tion	in vo ca tion
ap pli ca tion	med i ta tion
ap pro ba tion	min is tra tion
av o ca tion	mod e ra tion
cal cu la tion	nav i ga tion
cel e bra tion	nom i na tion
con fir ma tion	ob li ga tion
con gre ga tion	ob ser va tion
con ster na tion	op e ra tion
con tem pla tion	per spi ra tion
con ver sa tion	prep a ra tion
cor po ra tion	pres er va tion
cul ti va tion	proc la ma tion
dec la ra tion	prov o ca tion
dem on stra tion	pub li ca tion
des o la tion	rec re a tion
dis pu ta tion	ref or ma tion
ed u ca tion	rep u ta tion
em u la tion	res er va tion
ex cla ma tion	rev e la tion
ex pec ta tion	sal u ta tion
ex pli ca tion	sep a ra tion
gen e ra tion	sup pli ca tion
hab it a tion	trans por ta tion
im it a tion	trib u la tion
	val u a tion

THE UNITED STATES'

SPELLING BOOK,

WITH

APPROPRIATE READING LESSONS

BEING AN EASY STANDARD

FOR

SPELLING, READING AND PRONOUNCING

THE ENGLISH LANGUAGE,

ACCORDING

TO THE RULES ESTABLISHED BY JOHN WALKER,

IN HIS

CRITICAL AND PRONOUNCING

DICTIONARY.

BY SUNDRY EXPERIENCED TEACHERS.

Where now the thorn or tangled thicket grows,
The wilderness shall blossom as the rose.—*Humphreys.*

SIXTH EDITION—ENLARGED.

PITTSBURGH,
PRINTED & PUBLISHED BY CRAMER, SPEAR & EICHBAUM,
AND SOLD AT THE FRANKLIN HEAD BOOKSTORE,
IN MARKET, BETWEEN FRONT AND
SECOND STREETS.
1813.

The title page for "The United States Spelling Book" of 1813 notes that the rules are based on those of John Walker. The frontispiece lists a few word syllables. Pittsburgh, sold at the Franklin Head Bookstore.

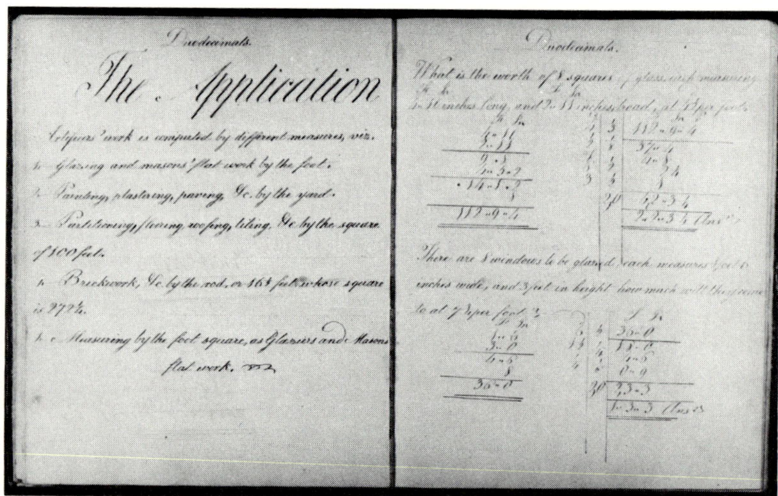

Duodecimals.

The Application

Artificers' work is computed by different measures, viz.

1. Glazing and masons' flat work by the foot.
2. Painting, plastering, paving, &c. by the yard.
3. Partitioning, flooring, roofing, tiling, &c by the square of 100 feet.
4. Brickwork, &c. by the rod, or 16½ feet whose square is 272¼.
5. Measuring by the foot square, as Glaziers and Masons flat work.

Duodecimals.

A boy's arithmetic exercise book from 1818 displays the emphasis placed on penmanship.

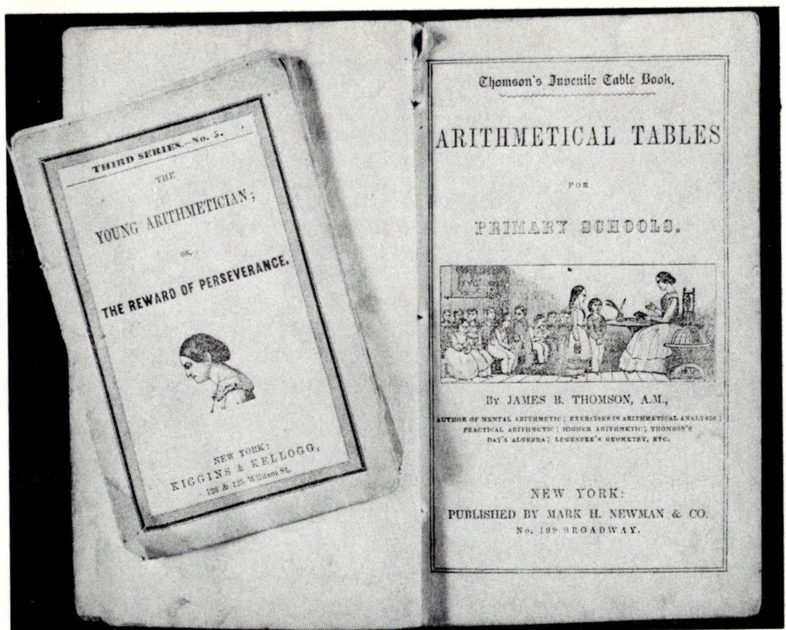

Arithmetic tables often took the form of a chapbook, and other softbound toybooks dealt with the reward of perseverance. Left: "The Young Arithmetician," circa the 1840's, Kiggins & Kellogg, New York. Right: "Thompson's Juvenile Table Book," 1848, Mark H. Newman & Co., New York.

surroundings as shown in the detail of the cuts accompanying his 1818 version of, "Aesop's Fables." At a later 1870's date, Louis Prang offered six volumes of color plates illustrating everything from "scratching" birds to "hornless" ruminants in his "Natural History Series for Children," by Norman Calkins and Mrs. A.M. Dias. A personal favorite on this subject is, "A Week Spent in a Glass Pond by the Great Water Beetle," written by J.H. Ewing in the 1880's with depictations by R. Andre. The story revolves around the adventures of some insects when they meet with children. Such a technique is still used today, that of incorporating scientific facts within a pleasant tale.

At the turn of the 19th century, a multiplicity of spelling books had inundated the schools of America. Many were based on "Walker's Critical and Pronouncing Dictionary," which formed the basis for, "The United States Spelling Book," first published in 1809. But the typical spelling book was more than a dictionary, for it usually contained geographical tables, an American Chronology of Events, poems, maxims, and the invariable religious teachings. "The United States Spelling Book," that was determined to utilize only the basics in instruction, included all of the aforementioned material in its 156 pages, but had only three pages devoted to grammar usage. Of course, it should be noted that many books of an instructive nature had to cover a multitude of information so that the author could sell copies to schools that had to be selective in their purchases.

By the 1860's, the geographical and event tables had been eliminated and replaced with lessons regarding syllable

Besides reading books, children utilized writing books to tabulate and practice their skills. Top: Eclectic Writing Speller, 1877. Bottom: Ellsworth Reversible Writing Book, 1877.

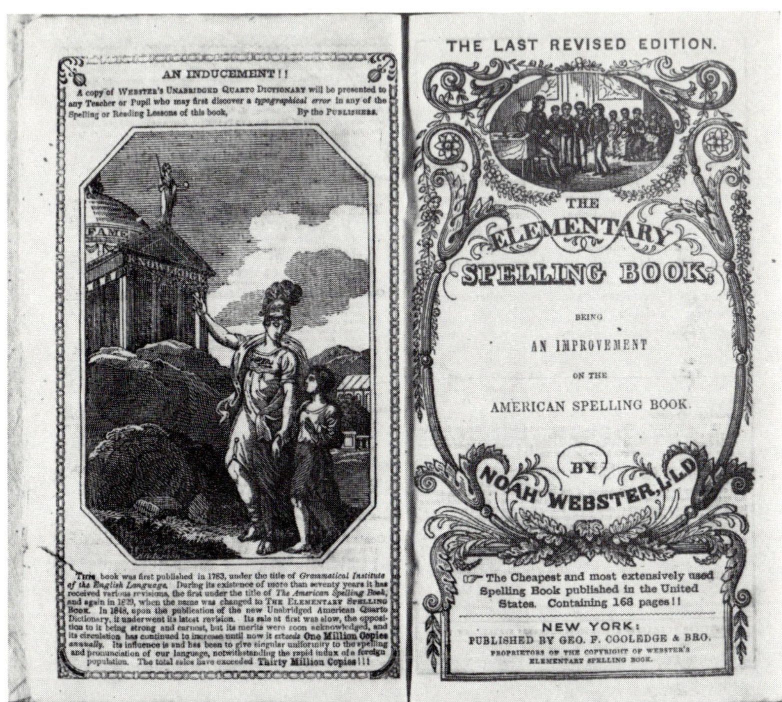

AN INDUCEMENT!!

A copy of Webster's Unabridged Quarto Dictionary will be presented to any Teacher or Pupil who may first discover a *typographical error* in any of the Spelling or Reading Lessons of this book, By the Publishers.

FAME

This book was first published in 1783, under the title of *Grammatical Institute of the English Language.* During its existence of more than seventy years it has received various revisions, the first under the title of *The American Spelling Book,* and again in 1829, when the name was changed to The Elementary Spelling Book. In 1848, upon the publication of the new Unabridged American Quarto Dictionary, it underwent its latest revision. Its sale at first was slow, the opposition to it being strong and earnest, but its merits were soon acknowledged, and its circulation has continued to increase until now it *exceeds* **One Million Copies** *annually.* Its influence is and has been to give singular uniformity to the spelling and pronunciation of our language, notwithstanding the rapid influx of a foreign population. The total sales have exceeded **Thirty Million Copies!!!**

THE LAST REVISED EDITION.

THE ELEMENTARY SPELLING BOOK; BEING AN IMPROVEMENT ON THE AMERICAN SPELLING BOOK.

BY NOAH WEBSTER, LL.D.

☞ The Cheapest and most extensively used Spelling Book published in the United States. Containing 168 pages!!

NEW YORK:
PUBLISHED BY GEO. F. COOLEDGE & BRO.
PROPRIETORS OF THE COPYRIGHT OF WEBSTER'S ELEMENTARY SPELLING BOOK.

According to the frontispiece of the 1848 version of Noah Webster's, "The Elementary Spelling Book," the first edition was published in 1783 under the title of "Grammatical Institute of the English Language." A dictionary was offered as a prize to anyone finding a typographical error in the last revised edition.

usage. "Willson's Larger Speller" of 1864 adopted, " . . . the orthography and pronunciation of Dr. Webster, as contained in the university edition of his Dictionary, edited by Prof. Goodrich." One may wonder as to how Dr. Webster would have felt about being associated with Peter Parley, the pseudonym of S.G. Goodrich.

The speller's prime competition came from the readers, such as Sanders or McGuffey's and the primers, as, "The Union Pictorial Primer." The numerous engravings used in these books made them more attractive to children and soon eliminated the need for a separate spelling volume.

Although not as glamorous as a "McGuffey's Eclectic Reader," a child's meager supply of school books also contained the invariable arithmetic book. Day and Thomson published a mathematical series in the 1840's which included tables, mental arithmetic, the principles of cancellation, algebra, geometry, trigonometry, and even an edition dealing with the elements of surveying. To a collector, the tables offer unusual

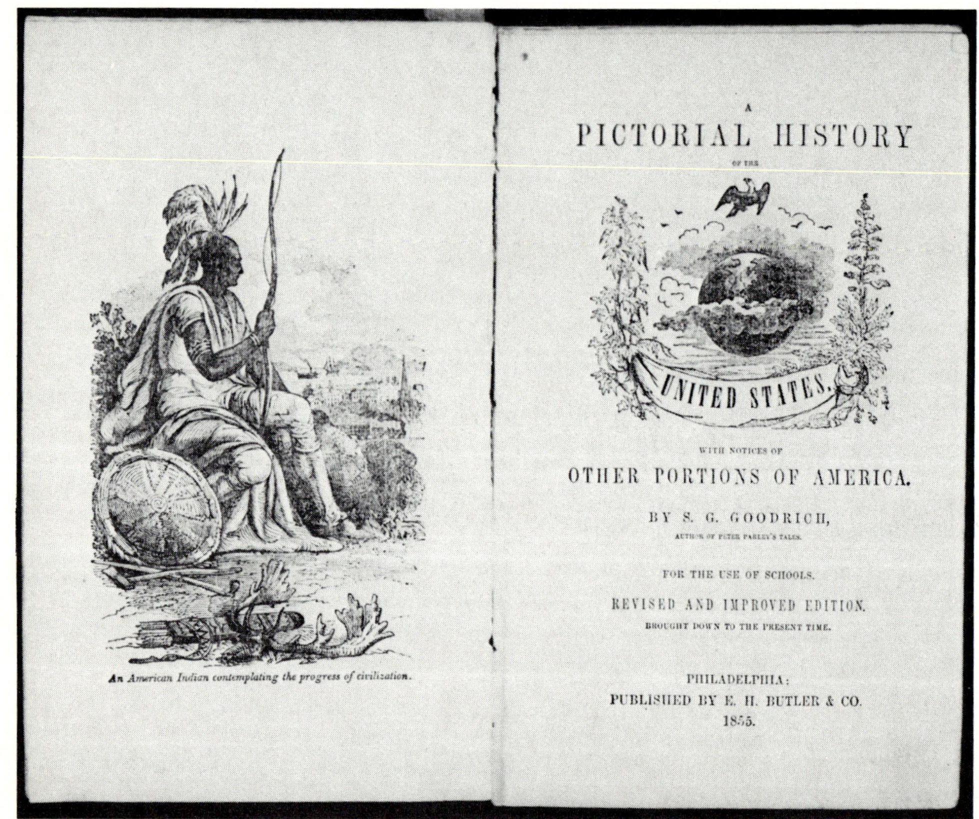

An American Indian contemplating the progress of civilization.

A
PICTORIAL HISTORY
OF THE
UNITED STATES,
WITH NOTICES OF
OTHER PORTIONS OF AMERICA.
BY S. G. GOODRICH,
AUTHOR OF PETER PARLEY'S TALES.
FOR THE USE OF SCHOOLS.
REVISED AND IMPROVED EDITION.
BROUGHT DOWN TO THE PRESENT TIME.
PHILADELPHIA:
PUBLISHED BY E. H. BUTLER & CO.
1855.

"A Pictorial History of the U.S.," by S.G. Goodrich, featured an Indian frontispiece in 1855.

facts, such as the conversions of New York and Federal monies, beer measures, Troy and Apothecaries' weights.

How interesting it would have been if children a hundred years ago could have glanced through one of today's geography textbooks. They would discover new countries, personalities, and products. Likewise, when a collector reads an antique geography book, he makes similar discoveries. For instance, an 1823 geography listed Indian corn and pearl ashes as principle articles of "domestick produce" and General Washington was noted "reluctant" to obey the call of his countrymen to become president. Perhaps the children of today would be more interested in the study of our country's past if they could use early geography books in their classes.

McGuffey, Olney, Goodrich, and Peter Parley are familiar authors to collectors of geographies. As previously mentioned, Parley was the pseudonym of Samuel G.

A SCHOOL HOUSE.

In many early geographies, such as J. Olney's modern version, a child's world began with a description of his schoolhouse and the surrounding locality. New York, 1853.

Goodrich, although Rev. Charles A. Goodrich also edited American histories. The Peter Parley Tales were published in over one hundred different juvenile versions in the 1820—1850 period and were known for their question-and-answer style. The Parley books are sought after by collectors, particularly early editions.

Personalizations and illustrations were a welcome addition to the student's geographies, especially the engravings and woodcuts which fascinated the readers then, as they do today. J. Olney offered numerous illustrations of manners and customs in his "modern" geography of 1853. The cuts included an Arkansas prairie fire, North Carolina gold mines, and commencing a settlement in the Western States.

In the preface is a statement regarding the value of the subject in addition to the three R's; "The introduction of geography into common schools, as a regular branch of education, has of late years become nearly universal." It further states that formerly the science was available only to the higher classes, and Olney recommended starting geography teachings with the town in which a student lives. Such personalization or regional specializing, extended from the schoolroom to the town, county to the state and on to the rest of the world. The beginner student was thus taken into consideration, in direct contrast to an 1823 "History of the United States" that stated: "It is recommended to the teachers not to make a severe examination of a pupil, until the second or third time going through the book. This particularly should be observed in regard to young and backward pupils."

The height of enlightenment in the world seemed to be centered in England

XIII.—LEAV-ING AT-LAN-TA.

Even the titles of pictures from McLoughlin's "General Sherman, His Life and Battles" were noted in words of one syllable, New York, 1886.

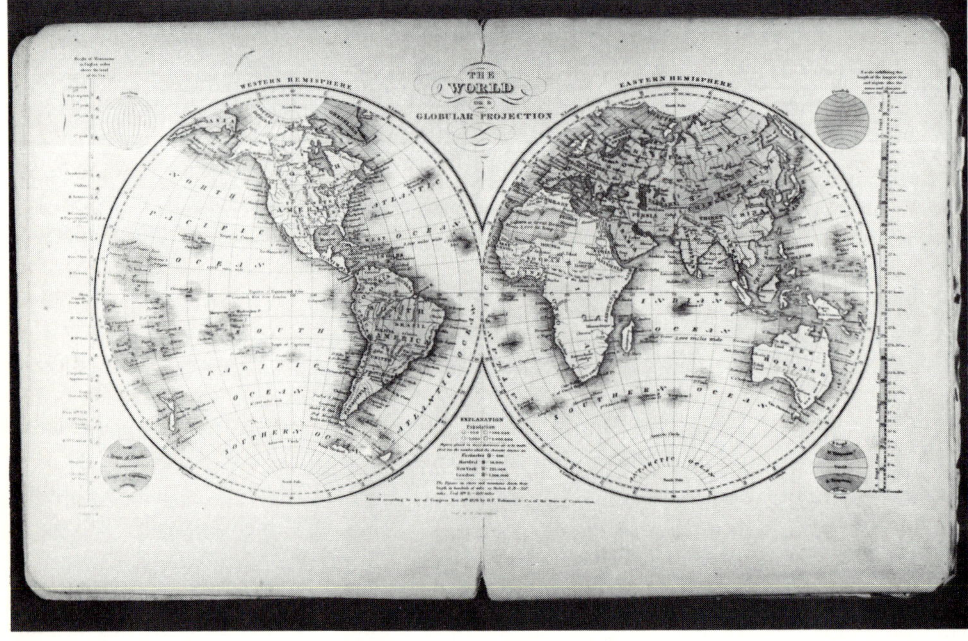

The world in an 1829 school atlas by J. Olney was quite different from today, with continents as New Holland and countries as Patagonia. Hand-colored engraving. (11½" by 19").

and the New England States. The Southern States were described in terms of trade or marketable produce, whereas the New England States usually had mention of famous people, educational facilities, and industrial centers. Unfortunately, the school children were not aware of any propaganda and memorized such statements as, "Charleston is more healthy than most Southern Cities." The territories-listed in 1844 as Florida, Wisconsin, Iowa, Mandan Indian, and Oregon—were given generous descriptions because of the interest in areas wild or newly explored.

In Roswell Smith's geography from this period, Indians were said to be indebted, "to the benevolent exertions of Christian missionaries." Text referring to massacres, savage life, and wild animals was added to spark a little interest in the subject, but contributed to a child's misconceptions about the Western wilds. Smith's edition also was accompanied in studies by a corresponding Atlas, as were many geographies in the early 1800's. It would be interesting for a collector to obtain such a set, for matching editions from this era could bring as much as $50 in an auction, depending on the author, maps, and condition. Maps are of particular interest, because location of boundaries, canals, forts, and railroads are usually given.

Generally, geographies of the pre-1830 period sell much higher than later 19th century editions. Any local or state geography from the period is desirable.

Children's books in the latter part of the Victorian era incorporated many of the techniques learned from the first readers, spellers, and geographies. Illustrations were of the utmost importance, as seen in Oliver Wendell Holmes' 1883 edition of "Grandmother's Story of Bunker Hill Battle," that featured colorful lithographs by H.W. McVickar. History was thus told in an enjoyable manner, without the burden of memorizing facts. McLoughlin Brothers relied on one of the elements of grammar to publish a series of popular books in the 1880's and 1890's. "Told in one-syllable words," was a key to their success, with topics ranging from "General Sherman His Life and Battles" to "The History of the United States."

Indeed, a child today could gain a great deal of knowledge from perusing the annals of instructive literature available in the 19th century, and perhaps, even form an appreciation for our country's struggle "to get the facts straight."

Rewards of merit were token cards given by teachers for diligence in reading or writing. Top: Two rewards circa the late 1860's. Bottom: Printed by L. Prang, 1867.

Related Books and Current Values

"Wilson's Book of Recitations and Dialogues," (As an assistant to students in preparing exhibitions) by Floyd B. Wilson, Dick & Fitzgerald publishers, N.Y., 1868, illustrated color cover, value $10.

"McGuffey's Eclectic Second Reader," by Wm. H. McGuffey, Winthrop B. Smith & Co., Cincinnati, 1853, illustrated, value $25.

"Arithmetical Tables for Primary Schools," by James B. Thomson, Mark H. Newman & Co., 199 Broadway, N.Y., 1848, pictorial paper covered boards, 4" x 6", value $10.

"Lessons for Little Readers," by B.D. Emerson, Hogan & Thompson, 30 N. 4th St., Philadelphia, value $5.

"Historical Amusement," Mark's Edition, Fisk & Little, 82 State Street, Albany, N.Y., circa 1850, paper wraps, value $15.

"The Flock of Sheep: or Familiar Explanations of Simple Facts," printed and published by S. Babcock, New Haven, 1840, 2¾" x 4½", pictorial yellow paper wraps, woodcuts, value $17.50.

"Museum of Foreign Animals or History of Beasts," printed and published by S. Babcock, New Haven, 1840, 2" x 3½", pictorial blue paper wraps, woodcuts, value $20.

"History of the United States No. VI or Uncle Philip's Conversations with the Children About New Hampshire," two volumes, Harper & Brothers, 82 Cliff Street, N.Y., 1844, illustrated 4" x 6", value $20.

"A Pictorial History of the United States," by S.G. Goodrich, published by E.H. Butler & Co., Philadelphia, 1855, illustrated, value $22.

"A History of the United States of America on a Plan Adapted to the Capacity of Youth," by Rev. Charles A. Goodrich, 2nd edition, published by Blake, Cutler and Co., Bellows Falls, Vt., 1832, engravings, value $20.

"Parley's First Book of History," Boston: Hickling, Swan and Brewer, Cleveland: Ingham and Bragg, 1859, engravings and hand-colored maps, value $18.

"Biographical Amusement," Mark's Edition, published by Fisk & Little, 82 State Street, Albany, N.Y., paper wraps, value $15.

"Frost's Dialogues for Young Folks," published by Dick & Fitzgerald, N.Y., 1868, value $6.

"A Practical System of Modern Geography or a View of the Present State of the World," by J.Olney, published by Pratt, Woodford & Co., N.Y., 78th edition, 1853, pictorial board covers, engravings, value $15.

"Smith's Geography on the Productive System," by Roswell C. Smith, published by John Paine, Hartford, 1844, value $12.

"The Eventful History of the Mutiny of the Bounty," Harper's Family Library No. XXI, by John Barrow, J. & J. Harper, 82 Cliff Street, N.Y., 1833, frontispiece engraving, value $35.

"Conversations on Common Things, or Guide to Knowledge with Questions," by a Teacher, 7th edition, Munroe and Francis, 128 Washington Street, Boston, 1837, pictorial paper board cover, value $18.

"New and Improved School Atlas," by J. Olney, published by Robinson, Pratt & Co., N.Y., 1837, pictorial paper board covers, hand-colored maps, value $30.

"Mitchell's School Atlas," revised edition, Thomas Cowperthwait & Co., Philadelphia, 1839, pictorial paper board covers, hand-colored maps, value $30.

"A Week Spent in a Glass Pond by the Great Water Beetle," by J.H. Ewing, published by R. Worthington, 770 Broadway, N.Y., color illustrations by R.Andre, value $18.

"The History of the United States—Told in One Syllable Words," by Miss Josephine Pollard, McLoughlin Brothers, N.Y., 1884, color illustrations, value $15.

"Grandmother's Story of Bunker Hill Battle," by Oliver Wendell Holmes, published by Dodd, Mead & Co., 756 Broadway, N.Y., 1875, color illustrations by H.W. McVickar, value $20.

"The United States Spelling Book," by Sundry Experienced Teachers, 6th edition, printed and published by Cramer, Spear & Eighbaum and sold at the Franklin Head Bookstore, Front & 2nd Streets, Pittsburgh, 1813, value $22.

"Sanders' Series, The School Reader," by Charles W. Sanders, published by William H. Moore & Co., 110 Main Street, Cincinnati, 1840, illustrated, value $10.

"The Union Pictorial Primer," by Charles W. Sanders, Ivison, Blakeman, Taylor and Co., N.Y. and Chicago, 1879, numerous illustrations, pictorial paper board covers, value $15.

"Willson's Larger Speller," by Marcius Willson, Harper & Brothers, N.Y., 1864, pictorial covers, illustrated, value $10.

"Introductory Course of Natural Philosophy," by William G. Peck, Barnes & Burr, 51 & 53 John St., N.Y., 1863, numerous illustrations, value $18.

"The History of the Pirates," published by Henry Benton, Hartford, 1829, woodcut frontispiece, value $30.

"General Sherman, His Life and Battles—In Words of One Syllable," by Mrs. Ida B. Forbes, McLoughlin Bros., N.Y., with 96 etchings by Edwin Forbes, 1886, value $20.

"Kendall's Uranography, or a Description of the Starry Heavens," by E. Otis Kendall, published by E.H. Butler & Co., Philadelphia, 1855, nine engravings, value $25.

"The Elementary Spelling Book," by Noah Webster, the last revised edition, published by Geo. F. Cooledge & Bros., New York, illustrated frontispiece and title page, advertisements, illustrations, 1848, value $20.

When opened, "A Rare Cat," reveals a four-layered pop-up scene with accompanying story text.

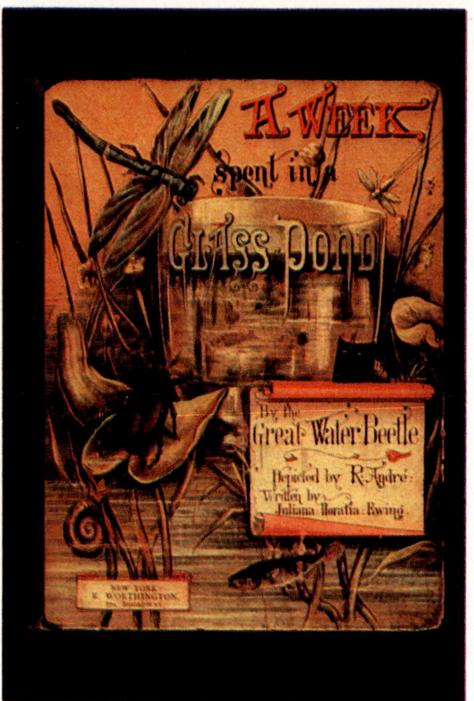

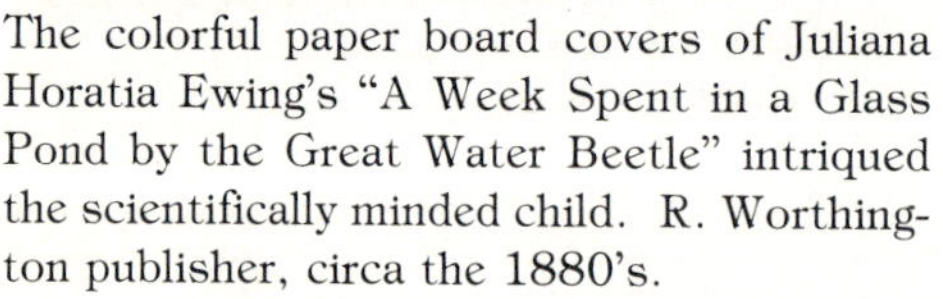
The colorful paper board covers of Juliana Horatia Ewing's "A Week Spent in a Glass Pond by the Great Water Beetle" intriqued the scientifically minded child. R. Worthington publisher, circa the 1880's.

In the preface of this book the publisher states that, ". . . Books on natural history have the first place in the hearts of Children." McLoughlin Bros., New York, 1886. (8½" by 11").

The talented L. Clarkson wrote, as well as illustrated "Buttercup's Visit to Little Stay-at-Home," a story that portrayed children as flowers and fields as fairylands. New York: E.P. Dutton & Co., 1881. (9¼ by 15").

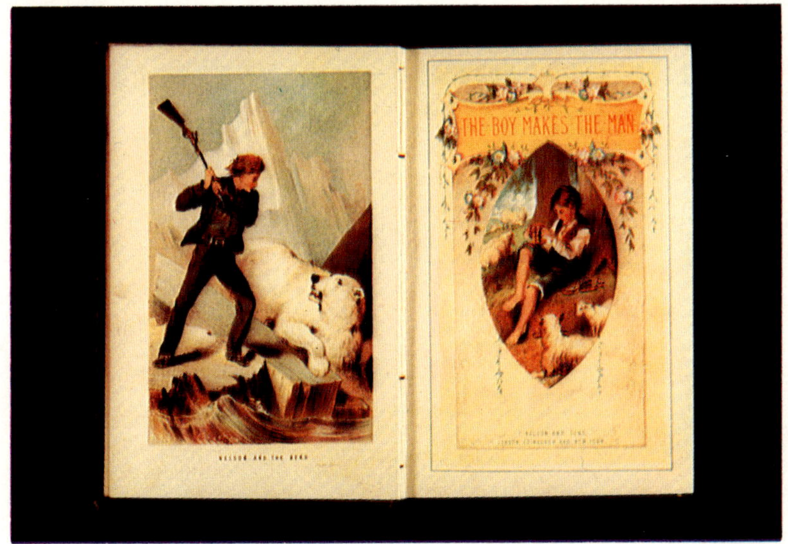

Color plates used as a title page or frontispiece can add value to a book, as in this 1873 edition of "The Boy Makes the Man."

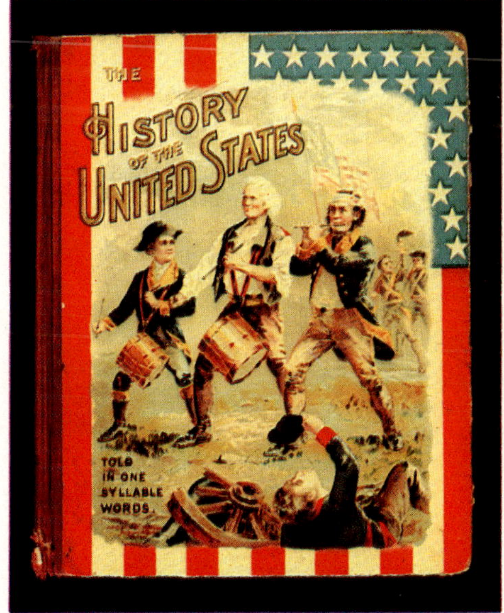

Books told in one-syllable words formed a series published by McLoughlin in the 1880's. The pictorial board covers are particularly attractive. New York, 1884. (7″ by 9″).

Almost every child in the latter part of the 19th century had a scrapbook that contained trade cards, greetings, calling cards, and pictorial scraps.

That perfectly well the
little shoe fit,
I know won't
astonish my
readers a bit;
Of course, 'twas her
own golden slipper
we know,
And on bended knee
did the young
Prince go.

And he begged
Cinderella to be
his wife,
To share his state
and make happy
his life;
While she her
wonderful story
told,
Of the fairy-queen
and the carriage
of gold.

And lastly, she
promised the
Prince to wed,
On his great horse
he took her; then
off they sped,
Away to the castle,
high up on the
hill,
Away from ashes
and tempers ill.

And all children I'm
sure, will be glad
to hear,
That Cinderella was
perfectly dear;
Her evil sisters she
fully forgave,
And as a Queen she
proved generous
and brave.

Colored paper honeycombs were added to give a three-dimensional affect to this B. Wilmsen version of Cinderella. Circa the 1880's, printed in Germany. (7½" by 10½").

A pantomime book of the 1880's had small pages attached to a larger chromolithographed stage, so that when the pages were flipped, the settings would change. "Bluebeard" was published by McLoughlin Brothers.

Title page to the first American version of "Under the Window," McLoughlin Bros., New York, 1878.

In Randolph Caledecott's color sketch from "The Babes in the Woods," a classical style is combined with fluid lines. London: Frederick Warne & Co. Ltd, printed by Edmund Evans, circa the late 1870's.

"Gulliver's Travels" was just one of the popular fairy tales in McLoughlin's Aunt Fanny's Series in the late 1850's.

A hand-colored illustration from "Gulliver's Travels" featured a decorative border, circa the late 1850's.

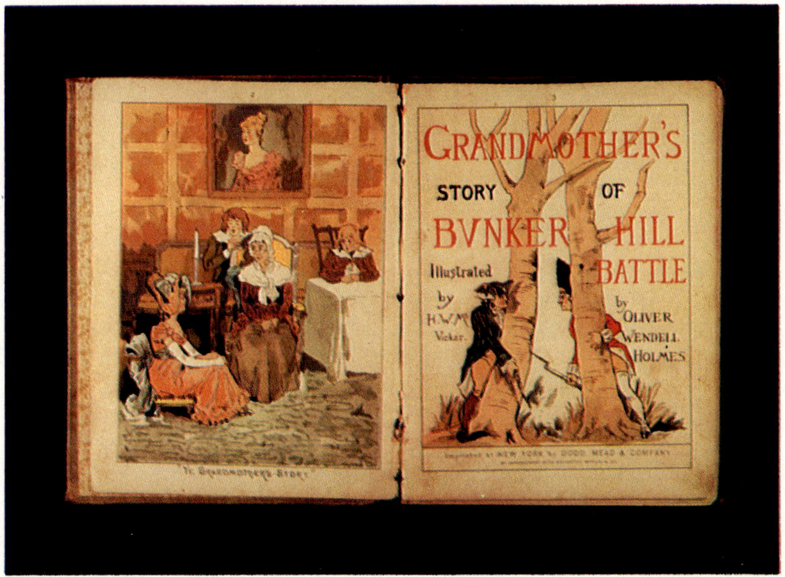

"Grandmother's Story of Bunker Hill Battle" was vividly illustrated by H.W. McVickar and written in verse by Oliver Wendell Holmes. New York: Dodd, Mead & Co., 1883. (9″ by 13½″).

The frontispiece to "Easy Lessons for the Little Ones at Home" displays an early attempt at chromolithography, circa 1870, 5″ by 6″.

"Pretty Stories for Children," an illuminated edition circa the 1860's, published by Philip J. Cozans of New York, approximately 4″ x 6″, hand-colored title page.

In this tale of the "History of Little Red Riding Hood" the wolf tore poor grandma to pieces, "To make of a poor harmless Lady a Feast." Hand-colored plates, circa the 1840's, Mark's Edition, Albany, New York, 4½″ by 7″.

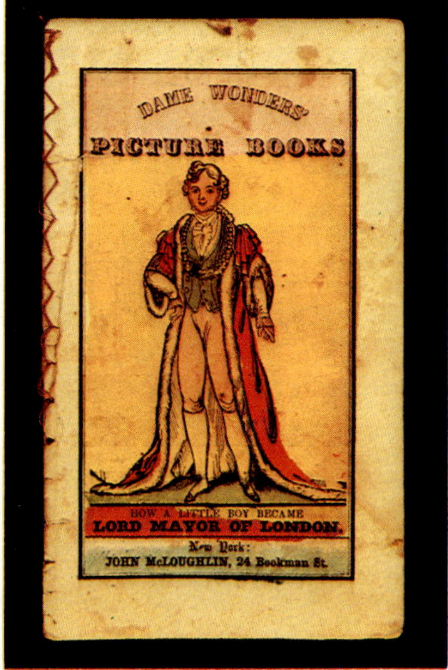

A softbound chapbook from the late 1840's entitled, "Dame Wonders' Picture Books," displays a handcolored woodcut for its title page. McLoughlin Brothers began producing toybooks in 1848. (4″ by 6″).

Chapter 4

Alphabet Basics

"If children would instruction get,
They first must learn the ALPHABET;
To easy words they then must go,
Until by heart each word they know:
To longer words they then proceed,
And thus in time learn how to read."
—From The Farmer Boy's Alphabet, circa 1860's

There is some question as to whether alphabet books have always been written for language instruction, or for that matter, for solely the use of children. Certainly the first primers were used as much for religious instruction as for learning the rudiments of language; even their origin lies in the church's "Book of Hours." Alphabet books have been around since the 16th century when "The B.A.C. Book in Latyn and in Englysshe" was printed in 1538 by T. Petyt of London.

Later, the alphabet was adapted to historical, moral, eventual, botanical, and zoological instruction. In fact, the alphabet book developed to such an extent in the latter part of the 19th century that it was used only as a framework for an artist's illustrative techniques, and in other cases, to facilitate the telling of nonsensical rhymes.

An adult or tutor seems to have been an invisible presence when most of the alphabet books were printed, for the text that accompanies the letters is far beyond the basics expected of a child. Undoubtedly, a parent was supposed to drill a child with alphabet exercises and any related rhymes before he attended school.

Although the accompanying rhymes usually had some connection with the letters individually discussed on each page, the woodcut or engraving shown above the rhyme frequently was a stock design. Thus, a printer had the opportunity to add a new alphabet toybook to his line without much bother. He only had to find enough cuts to reach twenty-six, for verses could be adapted to most any illustration. Such an attitude shows the importance placed on alphabet books in the first part of the 19th century.

To add more confusion to the learning process, much importance seems to have been placed on a child to learn the "syllabarium." This consisted of a list at the beginning of a book of double letters, such as ff, fi, fk, ih, and ib, often written in italics beneath the capital letters of the alphabet. Syllables were also listed beneath the rhymes in the chap-

GERMAN SPELLING BOOK.

Das

Amerikanische A-B-C-Buch.

Kurze und leichte

Lautir- und Buchstabirübungen.

Bearbeitet für

die öffentlichen Schulen in Cincinnati

von

Germanus.

Cincinnati:

Verlag von A. E. Wilde.

317 Main Straße.

A German Spelling and ABC Book of 1854 utilized pictorial cuts from a McGuffey's Reader.

✝Aabcdefghijklmnopq
rſstuvwxyz& aeiou
ABCDEFGHIJK LMNOPQ
RSTUVWXYZ

aeiou	aeiou
ab eb ib ob ub	ba be bi bo bu
ac ec ic oc uc	ca ce ci co cu
ad ed id od ud	da de di do du

In the Name of the Father and of the Son, and of the Holy Ghoſt. *Amen.*

OUR Father, which art in Heaven, hallowed be thy Name, thy Kingdom come, thy Will be done on earth, as it is in Heaven. Give us this day our daily Bread, and forgive us our Treſpaſſes, as we forgive them that treſpaſs againſt us, And lead us not into Temptation, but deliver us from Evil. *Amen.*

A facsimile drawing of an 18th century American horn-book.

book alphabets, and certainly must have added only bewilderment to a small child who had formerly been eager to learn letters. But the study of syllables was evidently assumed to be the stepping stone to proper reading, for there seems to have been few simple readers for a child. From the alphabet books and primers he jumped to the classics and nursery stories, which certainly offered a difficult transformation, and incidently, vocabulary.

Noticeably, many of the alphabet books in the 1810 to 1850 period had difficult words to master in the letter rhymes. "The Lulu Alphabet," published in 1850 by Samuel Raynor of New York, contained complicated letter descriptions as, "H, For the Harp Alice played on 'Lang syne,' or, L, for the Lady in costly array." Obviously such rhymes were to be read by a parent or teacher, but there was probably many a child who was expected to commit to memory these unrelated rhymes, without retaining the meaning of the common usage of each letter.

Besides forming the basis for the "New England Primer," the alphabet came to the forefront in 18th century America through the form of the hornbook. Because the paper-wrapped alphabet books were easily torn and destructible, an enterprising individual devised an object consisting of paper, transparent horn, and wood that could be carried about without damage. A printed or handwritten sheet listing the capitals, small letters, Roman and italic type was fastened to a paddle-shaped piece of wood or leather and then covered with a thin sheet of horn. The horn had been soaked for awhile in water, split, the core removed, and then a thin layer of horn taken from the inside. After turning translucent, the horn was rimmed in copper and then tacked to the wood, which had a hole in the handle for stringing at the waist. Some hornbooks also contained numbers, a syllabary and most often, the Lord's Prayer.

The transparent horn may have offered protection from the elements, but not from the inventive minds of children. Many early prints in children's books show that the hornbook was a handy item to be used in game play and even, occasionally, for a weapon!

Attempts at creating indestructible alphabets, to be carried about, date from the 16th century in England when the first nine letters of the alphabet were

11

A
In Adam's Fall,
We sinned all.

B
Thy life to mend,
This Book attend.

C
The Cat doth play,
And after slay.

D
A Dog will bite
A thief at night.

E
An Eagle's flight
Is out of sight.

F
The idle Fool
Is whipped at school.

An Alphabet of Lessons for Youth.

A WISE son maketh a glad father, but a foolish son is the grief of his mother.

BETTER is a little with the fear of the Lord, than great treasure, and trouble therewith.

COME unto Christ, all ye who labor and are heavy laden, and he will give rest to your souls.

DO not the abominable thing which I hate, saith the Lord.

"The New England Primer" contained a guide to reading, the assembly's shorter catechism, and advice from the 16th century martyr, John Rogers, Philadelphia, late 19th century. (3½" by 6").

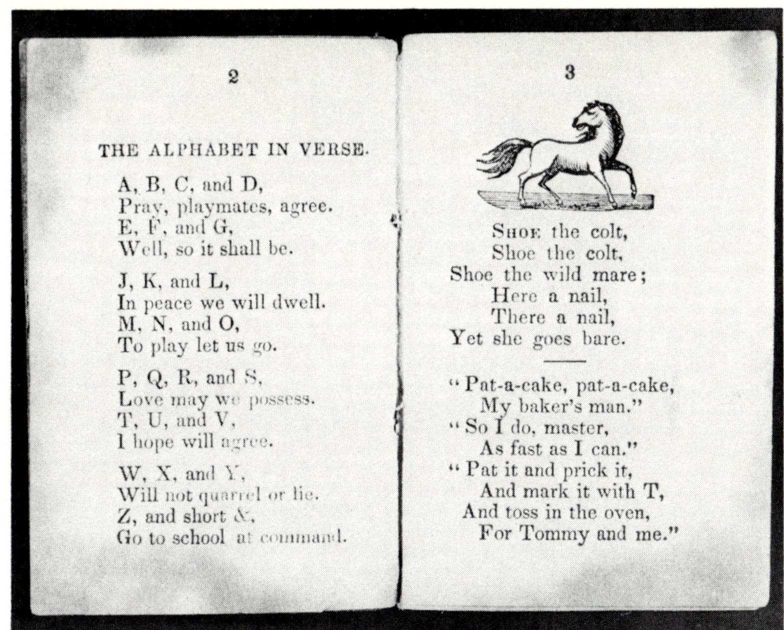

2

THE ALPHABET IN VERSE.

A, B, C, and D,
Pray, playmates, agree.
E, F, and G,
Well, so it shall be.

J, K, and L,
In peace we will dwell.
M, N, and O,
To play let us go.

P, Q, R, and S,
Love may we possess.
T, U, and V,
I hope will agree.

W, X, and Y,
Will not quarrel or lie.
Z, and short &,
Go to school at command.

3

SHOE the colt,
Shoe the colt,
Shoe the wild mare;
Here a nail,
There a nail,
Yet she goes bare.

"Pat-a-cake, pat-a-cake,
My baker's man."
"So I do, master,
As fast as I can."
"Pat it and prick it,
And mark it with T,
And toss in the oven,
For Tommy and me."

The alphabet in this verse ended with the statement, "Go to school at command." From "Rhymes for the Nursery," Kiggins & Kellogg, New York circa 1840's. (2¼" by 3½").

strung in bead-like fashion onto a wire cross. Known as the Christ cross or Chris-cross-Row, it combined instruction with prayer. Originally, prayer preceeded any lessons, and in some early hornbooks a small cross is in evidence at the top of the instructional sheet.

The church and politics entered into the world of children's literature, for in the period from 1538 to 1640, eight editions of ABC books were "liscensed" to be printed in England. These years are given only as an example, for the influence of the church continued throughout the alphabet prayers found in the "New England Primer" to the moral tracts of the 19th century.

The hornbook eventually fell by the wayside, due not only to its utilization in play, but also because there was a definite lack of space for lessons. The battledore became popular in the 18th century and consisted of a two-to-three-leaved card with printed lessons that folded into a pocketbook shape. Part of the printed sheet was pasted to the front leaf, forming a flap, and the whole affair was usually covered with "Dutch" flowered paper decorated with gilt. The battledore was made in both England and America and some examples featured hand-colored engravings or woodcuts accompanying the alphabet. The Lord's Prayer and other religious verses are noticeably absent from the battledore, the alphabet, numbers, and illustrations coming finally to the forefront. B. Johnson of Philadelphia printed battledores circa 1810's, but the largest English printer of them was Dean & Son who published battledores with verses as late as 1840.

Any discussion of alphabet books would not be complete without mention

The battledore became popular in the eighteenth century. Authentic examples are rare. Cover of "The Uncle's Present, A New Battledoor," published by Jacob Johnson, Philadelphia, circa 1810. Courtesy of Miami University Library, Oxford, Ohio, E. W. King Juvenile Collection.

Alphabet cards, such as these, provided children with a link between playtime and factual reading. Hand-colored, circa the 1860's, heavy cardboard, 4¼″ square.

of the origins of "A was an Apple Pie," or equally, "A was an Archer." Both of these alphabet verses date to at least the first part of the 18th century and are still in use today. "A was an archer, and shot at a frog," was one of two rhyming alphabets offered in a circa 1800 English version of "Tom Thumb's Play-thing." Other publishers of the rhyme include John Harris (1827), Richardson and Son (circa 1840), Benjamin Olds (1843), George Routledge & Sons (circa 1865), and Dean & Son (1867 or 1868.)

Perhaps the most popular edition of "A was an Apple Pie" was illustrated by Kate Greenaway in 1886 and published by G. Routledge & Sons. Her delightful children in bonneted and calico costumes adorned every page, and the color printing by Edmund Evans could not be surpassed. The advantage of "A was an Apple Pie" for children was that the rhymes were very short, as "B bit it, C cut it, D dealt it," and could be easily learned and recited. Mark's published a chapbook version of the rhyme in 1830 and Darton printed an "indestructible" Apple Pie circa 1860.

The rhyming alphabet books offering instruction in various fields of interest are full of little-known facts about the

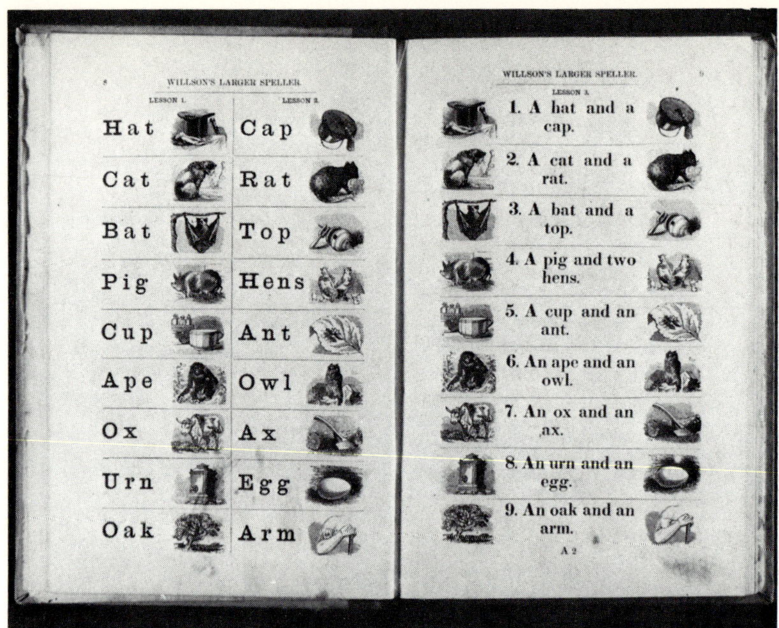

8 WILLSON'S LARGER SPELLER.

LESSON 1.	LESSON 2.
Hat	Cap
Cat	Rat
Bat	Top
Pig	Hens
Cup	Ant
Ape	Owl
Ox	Ax
Urn	Egg
Oak	Arm

WILLSON'S LARGER SPELLER. 9

LESSON 3.

1. A hat and a cap.
2. A cat and a rat.
3. A bat and a top.
4. A pig and two hens.
5. A cup and an ant.
6. An ape and an owl.
7. An ox and an ax.
8. An urn and an egg.
9. An oak and an arm.

A 2

Associating words with pictures was a common technique, as utilized in "Willson's Larger Speller" by Marcius Willson, New York, 1864. (4½" by 7¼").

times. For instance, McLoughlin Brothers printed an illuminated, "Farmer Boy's Alphabet or Speed the Plough" that was unique in its approach. The oil colored illustrations depicted incidents familiar to a farm boy as, "N shows the pleasant Nutting-time, and boys who love to ride and climb." The first lesson lists the vowels and then states, "After the child can name these and recognize them, he must be instructed to draw them on his slate; and the same must be observed in the other lessons." Besides the farming alphabet, paragraphs were given describing each rhyme as, "In the fall of the year boys go Nutting in the woods, and pick Blackberries from the bushes. Hogs and Deer seek acorns and Beechnuts in the forest." Such an approach elaborated the meanings of the letters, gave lessons in grammar, and facts familiar to the reader of the book.

Other alphabet books of instruction included "The Alphabet of Flowers"—1852; "The Picture Alphabet"—circa 1870, a book of religious psalms; "The Overland Alphabet"—1853, recounts a journey to India, and "The Picture Book of Birds"—1874. Perhaps these types of alphabet books are the most constructive for learning and certainly stimulated the mind of the child.

Constructive could not aptly be applied to the nonsensical alphabet rhymes, but such literature does contribute to a child's sense of lightheartedness. George Cruickshank, the early 19th century English comic illustrator, dabbled in alphabet rhymes, as well as the collectible Walter Crane who printed his "Absurd Alphabet" in 1874. Another collection of conundrums, obviously published for entertainment, was a J. Harris & Son 1820 version of, "Peter Piper's Practical Principals of Plain and Perfect Pronunciation." W.W. Denslow's alphabet book from the turn of the 20th century also treated the subject in a lighthearted vein,

The "Sanders' Union Pictorial Primer" was a favorite of teachers and sought to teach the names of letters before being introduced to a reader, New York, 1879. (4½" by 7").

but advertised, " . . . elimination of all coarseness, cruelty, and everything that might frighten children. Each book is filled with pictures of action and fun in brilliant colors." Children's literature had come a long way from the 19th century moral and religious-oriented primers.

McLoughlin Brothers was, again, the prime producer of alphabet books with some competition arising from Mark's toybooks, published in Albany, N.Y. Mark's printed examples as, "The Great Combination Alphabet," "The Illustrated A.B.C.D." and "Grandpapa Pease's Great Picture A.B.C." around the turn of the mid-century. Most of these toybooks had hand-colored woodcuts or engravings on the front and reverse of each page, whereas the majority of the McLoughlin alphabets dating from the 1870's, were color printed on one side only. Collectible McLoughlin paper wrapped books dating from the 1850's through the 1870's include, "History of an Apple Pie," "Amusing Alphabet," "Funny Alphabet," "The Child's First Book," "ABC of Objects," and "My First Alphabet." This publisher also manufactured the majority of ABC cards and blocks, which was undoubtedly another attempt at making the alphabet indestructible. The linen books of the latter part of the 19th century are evidence that printers continued the search for a material that would survive the rugged use of children.

A remarkable number of old alphabet books still remain to be discovered by collectors, proving that some children enjoyed, yet treasured, their possesions. Today they are treasured by their great-great-grandchildren, and hopefully, will be preserved for future generations.

Two popular alphabet books by McLoughlin Brothers were the "A.B.C. of Objects" and "Apple-Pie A.B.C."

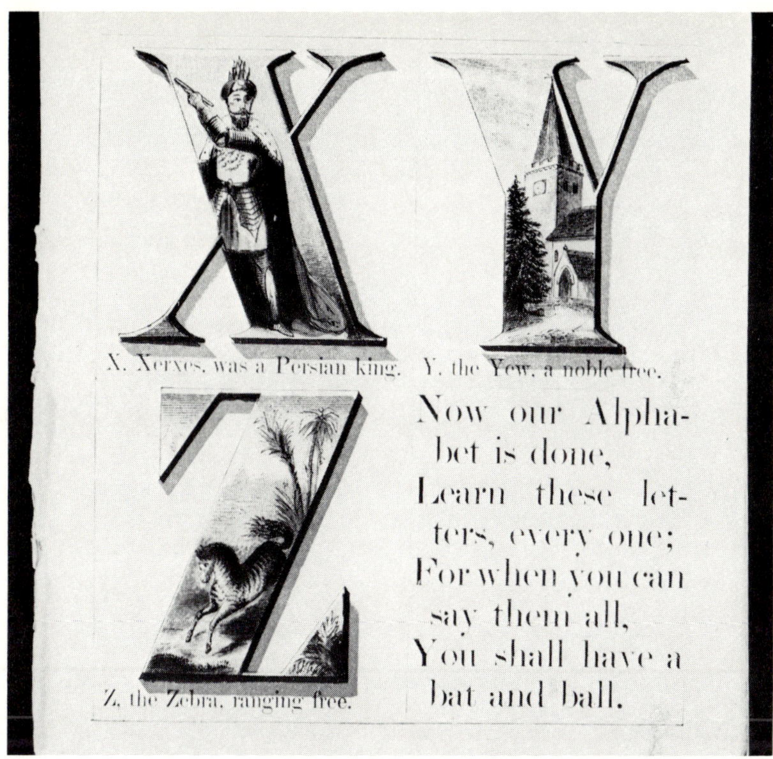

The "Alphabet of Objects" promised a bat and ball as a reward for learning all of the letters.

Related Books and Current Values

"Das Ameritanfche A-B-C Buch," A German Spelling Book, by Winthrop B. Smith, published by B. Wilde, 317 Main Street, Cincinnati, 1854, illustrated wraps, wood engravings taken from McGuffey's Eclectic Series. Value $7.50.

"Uncle Frank's Funny Alphabet," McLoughlin Bros., 24 Beekman St., N.Y., heavy paper wraps, circa 1860's, colored illustrations, value $8.

"The Picture Alphabet," in prose and verse, published by the American Tract Society, 150 Nassau St., N.Y., circa 1860's, value $5.

"Child's First Book," mammoth colored toy books, published by McLoughlin Bros., 24 Beekman St., N.Y., circa 1850's, value $12.

"Dame Wonders Amusing Alphabet," published by McLoughlin Bros., 24 Beekman, St., N.Y., circa 1860's, value $10.

"The Farmer Boy's Alphabet or Speed the Plough," published by Hurd and Houghton, 459 Broome St., N.Y., illustrated paper wraps, illuminated color lithographs, circa 1860's, value $12.

"Grandpapa Pease's Great Picture ABC," Mark's Toy Books, published by Fisk & Little, 82 State St., Albany, N.Y., circa 1850's, illustrated paper wraps, 4" x 6", value $15.

"Mother Goose ABC," Watts Songs, London, paper wraps, color lithographs, circa 1880's, 5" x 6", value $6.

"Aunt Effie's History of an Apple Pie," published by McLoughlin, 24 Beekman St., N.Y., illustrated paper wraps, hand-colored illustrations circa 1850's, value $15.

"Fancy Illustrated Alphabet," Mark's Toy Books, published by Fisk & Little, 82 State St., Albany, N.Y., circa 1850's, paper wraps, hand-colored illustrations, value $15.

"Large Letters for the Little Ones," published by Hurd and Houghton, 459 Broome St., N.Y., color paper wraps, oil colors, tinted paper, circa 1870's, value $10.

"Album of Fancy Alphabets," for designers, Excelsior Publishing House, 29 & 31 Beekman St., N.Y., quarto volume, circa 1900, value $8.

"My First Alphabet," published by McLoughlin Bros., 24 Beekman St., N.Y., six full-page color illustrations, circa 1870's, value $8.

"Great Combination Alphabet," Mark's Toy Books, published by Fisk & Little, 82 State St., Albany, N.Y., paper wraps, illustrated, circa 1850's, value $12.

"Aunt Mavor's Series-Picture Alphabet," published by McLoughlin, 24 Beekman St., New York, N.Y., paper wraps, hand-colored illustrations, circa 1850's, value $15.

"Picture Alphabet," by W. Walker, published by Otley, paper wraps, 1830, value $10.

"Ida Waugh's Alphabet Book," verses by Amy E. Blanchard, printed by J.B. Lippincott Co., 715 & 717 Market St., Philadelphia, two colors, illum. cover, 9" x 11", 1887, value $20.

"Alphabet of Farm-Yard," published by McLoughlin, quarto, six color illustrations, circa 1880's, value $10.

"Illustrated A.B.C.D.," Mark's Toy Books, published by Fisk & Little, 82 State St., Albany, N.Y., paper wraps, hand-colored illustrations, circa 1850's value $15.

"Nursery Rhymes ABC," Deans Gold Medal Series, #11, published by Dean & Sons, 160a Fleet St., London, 12" x 10", illustrated, 1890, value $18.

"Alphabet in Rhymes," published by McLoughlin, N.Y., quarto, paper wraps, six color illustrations, circa 1880's, value $8.

"Apple-Pie A.B.C.," McLoughlin Bros., Inc., Springfield, Mass., color lith., circa 1900, value $6.

"The History of an Apple Pie," London: Darton & Clark, colored plates, circa 1840, value $40.

"A Apple Pie," by Kate Greenaway, published by George Routledge, eng. and printed by Edmund Evans, London, 8½" x 10¼", 1886, value $60.

"The Shilling Alphabet: Tom Thumb's," George Routledge & Sons, Broadway, Ludgate Hill, London, color illustrated, circa 1865, value $35.

"Routledge's Coloured ABC Book," 24 illustrations by Kronheim and others, London: George Routledge and Sons, Broadway, Ludgate Hill, N.Y.: 416 Broome St., contains four alphabets, circa 1873, value $30.

"Kate Greenaway's Alphabet," color illustrations by Kate Greenaway, London and New York: George Routledge, circa 1885, value $50.

"The Pretty Alphabet," London: Dean & Son, Papa-Please-Me Well's Series, hand-colored illustrations, 1857, value $20.

"Baby's Own Alphabet," by Walter Crane, London: George Routledge & Sons, Walter Crane's Toybooks, new series, eng. and printed in color by Edmund Evans after Walter Crane, 1874, value $65.

"Darton's Alphabet of Birds," illustrated by Harrison Weir, London: Darton & Co., 1858, value $35.

"Great A Little a, Bouncing B, and Other Rhymes," seventh series—Sixpenny Picture Books, published by Thomas Nelson and Sons, London, Edinburgh, and New York, color illustrations pictorial covers, 1877, value $18.

Diminutive beings permeated many stories, but one of the all-time favorites would have to be "Tom Thumb," from McLoughlin's Cinderella Series, New York, circa 1870. (6¼″ by 9½″).

Chapter 5

Collector's Favorites

"Of Parents bereft,
These poor Orphans did roam,
O'er the Hill and the Dale,
In search of a home.
Little Thomas he felt
To the ocean inclined,
His Sister to learning
Had bent her young mind."
—The History of Goody Two Shoes, circa 1850's.

Every collector of children's books has his favorites, whether it be an alphabet book illustrated by Kate Greenaway, a classic tale as "Little Red Riding Hood," or an artistic edition by the publisher Raphael Tuck. Others prefer to collect only geographies, Bibles, tracts, or those with a fancy binding. Whatever the attraction, children's literature encompasses such a wide variety of topics that one may comfortably find his own niche.

The classic tales have always been favorites, or they would not have become classics. Likewise, nursery rhymes have furnished reading matter for children for centuries, and the mysterious Mother Goose seems to be responsible for much of their popularity.

The model for this teller of tales in verse may have been a printing of "Mother Louse of Louse Hall," near Oxford, England. Due to miscopying or a purposeful mistake, John Payne Collier was the first to change the name of the celebrated 17th century ale-keeper to "Goose." Thus, the English version is said to predate C. Perrault's **"Contes de la Mere Oye,"** whose author was a French philosopher (1628—1703) and also the originator of another classic, "Bluebeard." Supposedly Perrault wrote his stories to amuse his small son, but one may wonder as to why he chose to immortalize Gilles de Laval, whose crimes of black magic and the slaying of children, formed the basis for the Bluebeard fairy tale.

Actually, the first accredited English version of "Mother Goose" was issued in 1729 by J. Pote of Charing Cross, although there is a popular legend that the character was an American lady living in Boston in the early part of the 18th century. Many English origins gave rise to the belief that the best nursery rhymes came from Oxford. Another well known nursery character that emanated from the same area was Sarah Catherine Martin's 1804 illustrated text of, "Old Mother Hubbard and Her Dog." This fourteen-verse nursery story was to be enjoyed by children for centuries, and the early comic versions were said to launch the prolific publication of nonsense verse.

America is supposedly the birth place of "Yankee Doodle" and Sarah Hale's, "Mary had a Little Lamb." There seems to be a great deal of controversy surrounding the origins of most nursery rhymes, and unfortuantely, some early editions containing examples are undated or misdated, which only compounds the problem. The study of nursery rhymes is today an accepted pastime and interesting propositions are always coming to light, as those asserting that certain nursery characters are based on actual people, as Jack Sprat who is said to have ridiculed an Archdeacon Pratt in the mid-17th century. There is no doubt that nursery rhymes were an easy target for political interpretations, for certainly the government held strict control over the publication of early children's literature.

John Newbery (1713–1767) of England is considered the first publisher to recognize the need for books entirely for children. Unlike his predecessors, he rejected the use of stock woodblocks and type and had illustrations designed specifically for each book. The Newbery books are the height of juvenile literature, the forerunners to all that followed and certainly a rarity in any bibliophile's collection. It is no wonder that the annual award in America for the best children's book is know as the Newbery Award.

Newbery published over twenty children's classics in his lifetime, including the "Little Pretty Pocket Book," "The Lilliputian Magazine," and "Goody Two Shoes." The latter contained all the elements necessary for a good children's story: colorful descriptions, suspense

Many adventure tales were prototypes of the "Robinson Crusoe" theme. From Father Tuck's Play and Pleasure Series, untearable linen, London, circa the 1890's.

and a happy ending. It is only logical that "Goody Two Shoes" would become a favorite of children one hundred and fifty years ago and continue to be a prized edition of collectors today. Some accredit the tale to Oliver Goldsmith who often contributed to publications of Newbery, but there is no doubt that much of the content can be historically documented. The earliest copy extant is a third edition of 1766, noting on the cover in typical Newbery style to, " . . . See the Original Manuscript in the Vatican at Rome, and the Cuts by Michael Angelo." Obviously, a sense of humor and ability to attract a reader's attention can also be attributed to John Newbery.

"Tom Thumb," "The Guy of Warwick," "Jack the Giant Killer," "Red Riding Hood," "Cinderella," and "Sanford and Merton" were all popular stories read by children of the American colonies. "Robinson Crusoe" and "Gullivers Travels" headed the list of adventure tales, which were later to spawn similar yearnings by Mark Twain and Kipling in their recordings of the prankish, but adventuresome, small boys.

Defoe's "Robinson Crusoe" has existed since 1719 and declared by some as the most popular piece of fiction. Certainly almost every book publisher of the 19th century reproduced the story, equally attractive with hand-colored woodcuts in the Mark's editions of the 1850's or the chromolithography of a McLoughlin's 1890's copy. Of course, the real attraction of Robinson Crusoe is that illustrations are not necessary, for the story contains the secret longings of every man, so that anyone can transport himself through imagination to the castaway island. Jules Verne also capitalized on man's ability to imagine fantastic surroundings, as in his 1875 masterpiece entitled, "The Mysterious Island", and Robert Louis Stevenson's "Treasure Island" of 1883 was undoubtedly based on a "Crusonian" desire.

"Gulliver's Travels" was created in a different vein, for Jonathan Swift carried the castaway island one step further into a land of allegories and science fiction, paving the way for the Jules Vernes and the yellow brick road of Frank Baum. It is interesting how themes were repeated throughout children's literature, certainly little people appeared or were inferred as readers in everything from a 1794 edition of "Tommy Thumb's Song Book" to William Donahey's "Teenie Weenie Neighbors" of 1945. Swift's

Samuel Croxall is credited with being one of the first to translate the "Fables of Aesop" into English. Frontispiece to the twelfth edition, London, 1782.

FABLE CLXXVII.

THE BULL AND THE GOAT.

A Bull being pursued by a Lion, fled into a cave where a Wild Goat had taken up his abode. The Goat upon this began molesting him and butting at him with his horns. "Don't suppose," said the Bull, "if I suffer this now, that it is you I am afraid of. Let the Lion be once out of sight, and I will soon show you the difference between a Bull and a Goat." Mean people take advantage of their neighbors' difficulties to annoy them; but the time will come when they will repent them of their insolence.

(176)

FABLE CLXXVIII.

THE BOY BATHING.

A Boy was bathing in a river, and, getting out of his depth, was on the point of sinking, when he saw a wayfarer coming by, to whom he called out for help with all his might and main. The Man began to read the Boy a lecture for his fool-hardiness; but the urchin cried out, "O, save me now sir! and read me the lecture afterwards."

(177)

An 1864 version of "Aesop's Fables" bore illustrations by John Tenniel of "Alice in Wonderland" fame.

1726 printing of travels, "By Lemuel Gulliver, first a surgeon, and then a captain of several ships," contained the exciting, "A Voyage to Lilliput." Gulliver's Travels became a standby for many publishers, as McLoughlin's printing in the 1850's as part of Aunt Fanny's Fairy Tale Series. Although the hand-colored illustrations are appealing and quaint, they cannot compare to the later line drawings of Arthur Rackham in an 1899 version.

Swift is considered by some as a fabulist, but there is no doubt that the age-old Aesop and his fables became the prototype for many followers. Aesop is as mysterious in origin as Mother Goose, and likewise, had many additions contributed by a variety of authors through the centuries. The fables had been in circultaion at least since the mid-part of the 5th century B.C. in Athens, Greece and his teachings were praised by the likes of Socrates, Plato, and Aristophanes. Most likely his accounts were at first oral, and so license to change the stories or to add morals was left to the recorder. Interesting 19th century examples of the fables include an 1860 version, "The Children's Picture Fable-Book" with sixty illustrations by Harrison Weir, which incidently, were engraved by John Greenaway, Kate's father. A Rev. James Thomas introduced his 1848 edition of "James' Fables of Aesop" with mention of his helpful illustrator, John Tenniel. Although this is not the first book to be illustrated by Tenniel, who later illustrated the unforgettable "Alice in Wonderland," it did cause "Punch" magazine to notice him.

It would be impossible to touch on all the collector's favorite children's books of the 19th century, for so many of them are treasured for personal reasons. Perhaps a book was a dog-eared copy of

Randolph Caledecott's picture books were admired for their irresistible humor, color illustrations, and outline sketches. Softbound cover of "Come Lasses and Lads," Frederick Warne & Co. Ltd, printed by Edmund Evans, London, circa the late 1870's.

Mother Goose Rhymes passed down through the family, or maybe an artist has an affinity for the illuminative and decorative style of editions illustrated by Walter Crane. Two artists in the latter part of the century do seem to be recognized by all bibliophiles attracted to children's literature; the delightful, yet idyllic, Kate Greenaway and the austere Victorian appearance of the Brownies creator, Palmer Cox.

As so often is the case, Kate Greenaway came from a family accustomed to the ways of publishing and illustrating. Her father was a wood engraver for such publications as "The Illustrated London News," that later published many of his daughter's designs. Her first drawings were exhibited in 1868, after winning medals for her illustrations at the Art Department of South Kensington, England and at other art schools. These fairy story drawings were later published in "People's Magazine" and other subsequent designs were printed as greeting cards for Marcus Ward & Co. Many of the early cards are missing the identifiable initials "K.G.," but the fairies and children among flowers usually label the design unmistakeably as Greenaways. Besides her card designs, magazine illustrations, and drawings to accompany other author's works, she illustrated over twenty-five books of her own. Perhaps her most popular work was the 1878 edition of "Under the Window," that launched her career with the well known color printer, Edmund Evans. Friend of Randolph Caledecott, admired by Walter Crane, likened to Rosetti, and advised by John Ruskin, Kate Greenaway deservedly was a legend in her own lifetime. It is sad that at the end of her life she believed

A children's classic, "Mother Goose or The Old Nursery Rhymes" was illustrated by Kate Greenaway in 1881. Engraved and printed by Edmund Evans, London: George Routledge. (6¾" by 4¾").

Palmer Cox, author of the Brownie stories, was a versatile individual who adapted his Brownies to advertising, plays, and products.

that she was no longer in fashion, and at her death in 1901, she had no idea of the following that was yet to come.

In a Kate Greenaway illustration of 1874 entitled, "A Christmas Dream," a sleeping child is surrounded by a myriad of mischievous tiny fairies. These fairies, who usually appear in the dark of night, are similar to those drawn by Palmer Cox in his Brownie stories. The Brownies were drawn from small, gremlin-like figures that Cox's Scottish relatives told him about when he was a child. Born in 1840, his family settled in Granby, Quebec near the United States border of Vermont, but at seventeen he left to visit the Eastern states and eventually drifted West to California. Some of his articles for the newspapers were illustrated, and he soon found that his writing played a subordinate part.

The Western papers did not offer much encouragement to a struggling illustrator, especially financially, so he returned East where there was a definite need for new artists. In 1875 he had his first book published in New York, entitled, "Squibs of California, or Every-day Life Illustrated." From that point, his output was nothing short of tremendous, completing

KING FLORIMEL GREETS THE PRINCESS.

Howard Pyle's stylized art nouveau drawings could be appreciated by adults as well as children. From "How the Princess's Pride was Broken," Harper's Young People, December, 1886.

"He dipped it into his cup of tea and looked at it again"

A Peter Newell illustration from a 1901 edition of "Alice in Wonderland."

a book every year and contributing simultaneously cartoons for "Life," "Wild Oat's," "Merriman's Weekly," "Wide Awake," "Little Folks," "Harper's Young People," and "St. Nicholas Magazine." Many of these comic drawings were of animals, especially quaintly dressed bears and foxes, that were also adapted in numerous advertisements.

The Brownies first appeared in an October 1882 issue of "St. Nicholas." Each successive story introduced a new

The Brownies invaded a number of localities, such as the children's schoolroom. St. Nicholas Magazine, October, 1885.

character, such as the Scotsman or Dude, until over fifty designs had been depicted. The only female figure was a nurse, who brandished the same rounded stomach and toothpick limbs. Supposedly, Theodore Roosevelt requested the Dude, which is indicative of the popularity that the imps achieved.

The Brownie books, detailing their mischievious adventures, were instigated by the 1887 edition of "The Brownies: Their Book," followed by at least sixteen books published in a series from 1887 through 1913. Palmer Cox had left his mark of the diminutive Brownies in the 1890's as much as Kate Greenaway had influenced illustration and fashion styles of the 1870's and 1880's. He died in 1924, a man who was known to have never flaunted even slightly a triumphant expression, yet in his lifetime was adaptable as an illustrator, advertiser, storyteller, poet, and playwright.

These storytellers, fabulists, illustrators, rhymers, and publishers have left us a tremendous heritage. It is now up to us to preserve their outpourings and to learn from their examples. The most inconsequential, tattered toybook could give us a clue to the past or be the last link to a forgotten origin.

The artist W.W. Denslow used a familiar character in his 1903 version of the "House That Jack Built." G.W. Dillingham Co., New York. (8½" by 11").

Related Books and Current Values

"Gulliver's Travels," Aunt Fannys Fairy Tale Series, published by Jno. McLoughlin, 24 Beekman St., N.Y., hand-colored plates, heavy paper wraps, circa 1860's, value $22.

"Under the Window After Kate Greenaway," McLoughlin, N.Y., undated first American edition, color engravings and cover, no K.G. signatures on plates, 1878, value $35.

"Mother Hubbard and Her Dog," 2nd Series Sixpenny Picture Books, Thomas Nelson and Sons, London, Edinburgh and New York, color illustrations, pictorial covers, 1877, value $18.

"The History of the Children in the Wood," Mark's Edition, published by E.H. Pease & Co., 82 State St., Albany, N.Y., hand-colored illustrations, softbound, 4″ x 6″, circa 1850's, value $25.

"Adventures of a Pioneer Boy While a Prisoner of War," by Alvan G. Bacon, private printing, Utica, N.Y., 32 pages, softbound, pictorial cover, 6″ x 8″, circa 1866, value $18.

"History of Goody Two Shoes," Uncle Frank's Series, McLoughlin Bros., 24 Beekman St., N.Y., softbound, hand-colored illustrations, illustrated wraps, circa 1860's, value $30.

"Dick Whittington and His Cat," versified by Mrs. Clara Doty Bates, illustrated by C.D. Finley, D. Lothrop & Co., Franklin and Hawley Sts., Boston, paper boards, color and gilt cover, 5″ x 6″, 1877, value $8.

"History of John Gilpin," McLoughlin Bros., N.Y., illustrated yellow wraps, hand-colored illustrations, 4″ x 6″, circa 1850's, value $25.

"The Word-Picture Fable Book, or Old Aesop in a New Dress," Thomas Nelson and Sons, London, Edinburgh and New York, color illustrations, gilt edges, 1877, value $20.

"The Jackdaw of Rheims," by Thomas Ingoldsby, Raphael Tuck & Sons, London, Paris & New York, printed at the Fine Art Works in London, heavy paper wraps, color cover, sepia illustrations, 6½" x 7", circa 1880's, value $18.

"The Book of Nursery Rhymes," with 16 color illustrations, designed by Alfred Crowquill, Thomas Nelson and Sons, London, Edinburgh and New York, ornamental boards, value $22.

"Life and Death of Cock Robin," published by E.H. Pease & Co., Mark's Toybooks, 82 State St., Albany, N.Y., softbound, hand-colored illustrations, 4" x 6", circa 1850's, value, $25.

"Aesop's Fables," complete, by Rev. T. James, J.B. Lippincott & Co., Philadelphia, with numerous engravings by John Tenniel, 1864, value $25.

"Sandford and Merton," by Thomas Day, revised by Cecil Hartley, eight illustrations by Herrick and others, published by Hurd and Houghton, 459 Broome St., N.Y., circa 1870's, value $18.

"History of Tom Thumb," 7th Series Sixpenny Picture-Books, Thomas Nelson and Sons, London, Edinburgh and New York, color illustrations, pictorial covers, $22.

"Rural Poems," by William Barnes, Robert Brothers, Boston, illustrated by Winslow Homer and Hammatt Billings, gilt edges, 1869, value $15.

"Valentine and Orson," Father's Series, McLoughlin Bros., New York, softbound, color cover and illustrations, 4" x 5", circa 1870's, value $18.

"The Frog Who Would a-Wooing Go." McLoughlin Bros., New York, Fairy Moonbeam's Series, printed in oil colors, color cover, softbound, circa 1870's, value $15.

"Dame Trot and Her Comical Cat," Mark's Toybooks, published by Fisk & Little, 82 State St., Albany, N.Y., hand-colored illustrations, softbound, 4" x 6", circa 1850's, value $20.

"Tom Thumb," Cinderella Series, McLoughlin Bros., N.Y., color illustrations and cover, softbound, 7" x 8", circa 1880's, value $12.

"The Three Little Kittens," Ninepenny Books, The Kitten Series by R.M. Ballantyne, Thomas Nelson and Sons, London, Edinburgh, and New York, colored frontispiece, numerous engravings, 1877, value $15.

"Yankee Doodle," Big Picture Series, McLoughlin Bros., New York, softbound, color illustrations, circa 1880's, value $20.

"Robinson Crusoe," Father Tuck's Play & Pleasure Series, published by Raphael Tuck & Sons, Co. Ltd., New York, London, Paris, color illustrated, untearable linen, circa 1890's, value $12.

"Famous Jingles," McLoughlin Bros., New York, hardback with color illustrations attached to cover, 48 color illustrations, circa 1870's, value $25.

"Life and Death of Jenny Wren," McLoughlin Bros., New York, Pleasure Book Series, softbound, color covers, circa 1870's, value $15.

"Under the Window," illustrated by Kate Greenaway, with colored pictures and rhymes for children by Kate Greenaway, eng. and printed by Edmund Evans, London: George Routledge, 9¼" x 7¼", 1878, value $100.

"Robinson Crusoe," Miss Merry-Heart's Series, McLoughlin Brothers, 24 Beekman St., N.Y., softbound, hand-colored illustrations, circa 1850's, value $27.

"Aesop's Fables, with Croxall's Applications," published by Hurd and Houghton, 459 Broome St., N.Y., 100 illustrations by H.W. Herrick, circa 1870's, value $15.

"Sing a Song of Sixpence," Ancient Illuminated Rhymes, McLoughlin Brothers, New York, softbound, oil color illustrations, circa 1860's, value $15.

"The Merry Adventures of Robin Hood," written and illustrated by Howard Pyle, Charles Scribner's Sons, N.Y., embossed leather binding, 1883, value $22.

"Blue Beard," Aunt Fanny's Fairy Tales, McLoughlin Bros., 24 Beekman St., N.Y., hand-colored illustrations, softbound, 6½" x 7", value $20.

"The Brownies: Their Book," by Palmer Cox, The Century Company, New York, green glazed boards, cover lettered in brown with orange and brown decorations, Brownies in orange, blue and brown; De Vinne Press seal below copyright notice, 1887, value $60.

T. W. Strong's circa 1820's chapbook, "Sports for All Seasons," had a hand-colored title page and featured illustrations of children's games and pastimes.

Chapter 6

Just For Fun

"The knowledge we derive from books,
As well delights the mind,
As strengthens it, and makes the wit,
And manners, too, refined."
—From, "Luke Lovebook," circa 1850.

There have always been adults who thought like children, and likewise, children who felt comfortable in an adult world. Thank goodness for the former, for without adults who cared to gain an insight into the confines of a child's imagination and potential intelligence, much of any thought provoking literature would have remained unwritten. There were others who realized that children deserved to have books written just for them, to be enjoyed again and again, and a moral lesson was not necessarily an attribute. Obviously, the moralist writers found this attitude difficult to overcome.

But what about the children who felt comfortable in an adult world? Some of the best loved stories, as "Alice in Wonderland," appealed to adults and children alike. The mazes and riddles interspersed in the book have attracted even scholars to determine their meanings, and any child capable of reading the story can find adult counterparts to the characters, such as the overbearing queen and the Mad Hatter.

Since the majority of the literature in the 18th century was written for adults, it is not surprising that children were attracted to such favorites as "Aesop's Fables", and relegated them to their own libraries. In fact, it seems that it was the children who demanded books written at their own level. The sudden surge of interest at the turn of the 19th century to produce so many toybooks is evidence of this demand.

Books with riddles or conundrums date to at least the mid-18th century, and again, were mainly written for adult

A

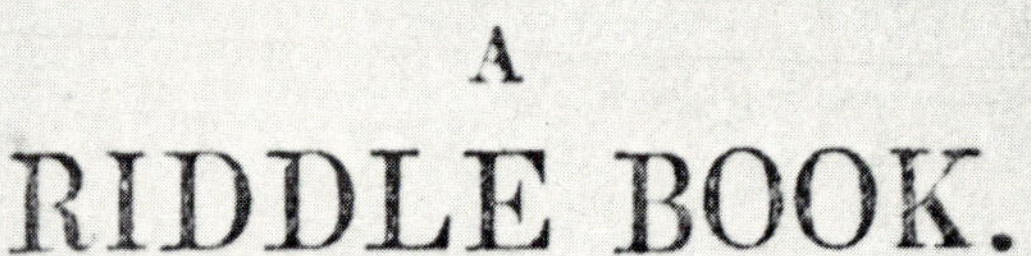

RIDDLE BOOK.

Come you that love riddles,
And guess them so well;
Now answer me all these,
For I know you can tell.

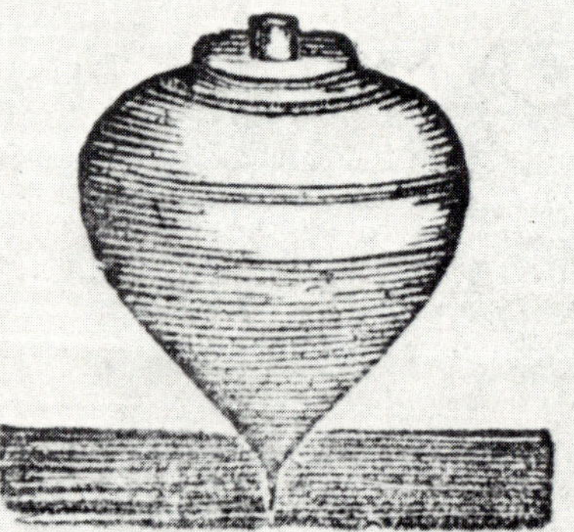

ERIE, PA.

PUBLISHED BY O. D. SPAFFORD,

1847.

This tiny riddle book of only 2¼″ by 3¼″ contained poems with accompanying woodcuts. The child had to guess what animal or object was being described. Published by O.D. Spafford, Erie, Pennsylvania, 1847.

111

83.

Rebus.

ILLUSTRATIONS OF PROVERBIAL PHILOSOPHY.

Riddles.

84. What is that we cannot buy with all the gold of the earth?

85. Pleasant is my food—sweet is the fruit of my labor, and dangerous is my revenge. Who am I?

86. In the spring I revive you—in summer I cool you—in autumn I nourish you—and in the winter I warm you.

87. What is that which makes every one sick but the one that swallows it?

88. What foreign letter makes the title of a noble lady?

89. What business would you advise a short-boy to engage in?

90. The figures representing my age, are what you ought to do in all things.

Early puzzle books, although popular, are quite difficult to find. As seen in "Puzzledom-An Original Collection of Charades, Conundrums, Puzzles, and Games." Philadelphia, 1866. (5¼" by 7¼").

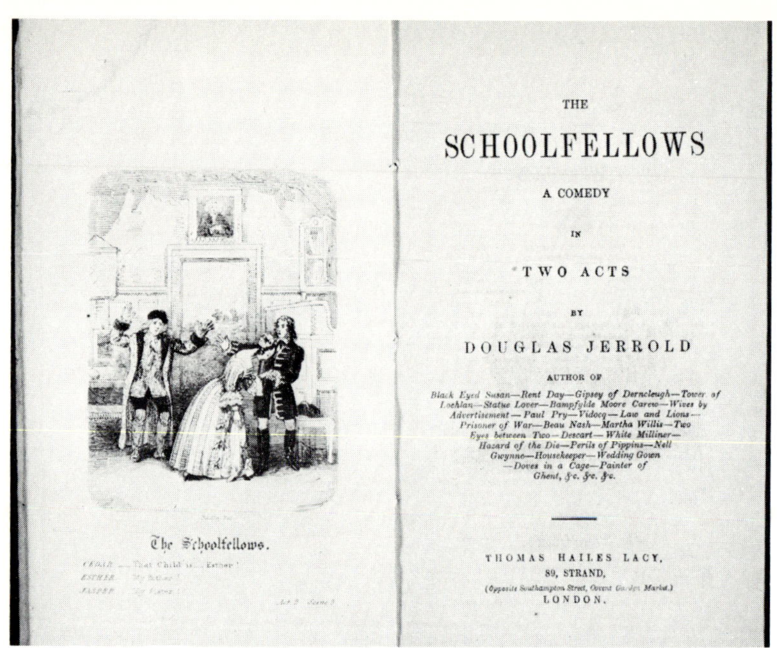

THE

SCHOOLFELLOWS

A COMEDY

IN

TWO ACTS

BY

DOUGLAS JERROLD

AUTHOR OF

Black Eyed Susan—Rent Day—Gipsey of Derncleugh—Tower of Lochlan—Statue Lover—Bampfylde Moore Carew—Wives by Advertisement—Paul Pry—Vidocq—Law and Lions—Prisoner of War—Beau Nash—Martha Willis—Two Eyes between Two—Descart—White Milliner—Hazard of the Die—Perils of Pippins—Nell Gwynne—Housekeeper—Wedding Gown —Doves in a Cage—Painter of Ghent, &c. &c. &c.

THOMAS HAILES LACY,
89, STRAND,
LONDON.

Plays were prevalent as a pastime both at home and on a stage. "The Schoolfellows," which was conceived in 1835 by Douglas Jerrold, contained a penciled notation by a student that it was, "heavy and stupid." London. (4″ by 7¼″).

amusement. But the toybooks that followed 50 years later usually had one of a series devoted to riddles, and this time, they were decidedly written with children in mind. J. Kendrew of York, England published, "A Collection of Birds and Riddles" circa 1820 which was simply a chapbook with woodcut illustrations to accompany the verses. The pseudonym Peter Puzzlecap was attached to other chapbooks in the 1830's, such as "Puzzlecap's Amusing Riddle Book" and "The Riddler's Riddle Book." The riddles based on double meanings had first been used in a circa 1765 publication entitled, "A New Riddle Book or A Whetstone for Dull Wits." Actually, the immediate popularity of the riddle books may have been one of the reasons why the question-and-answer style of text was later adopted by such authors as Peter Parley.

Another technique of writing verse that is age-old is the limerick. Supposedly, the well-known humorist, Edward Lear, received his inspiration from a circa 1820's version of "Anecdotes and Adventures of Fifteen Gentlemen." This edition, with hand-colored illustrations attributed to Robert Cruikshank, includes the limerick, "There was an old man of Tobago . . ." Lear realized from this short verse the innumerable possibilities of such a technique and his 1846 printing of "A Book of Nonsense" bears testimony to this influence. His book was a landmark, for it changed the attitudes of authors and publishers alike. It was now possible to publish a book solely for the purpose of enjoyment—no hidden messages, moral overtones, or facts to memorize. Reading could be fun!

THE

CHILDREN'S MAGAZINE.

Vol. X. MAY 1, 1838. No. 5.

The last Magazine gave the young reader an account of Lapland travelling, and of the goodness of God in providing food and clothing, and swift beasts to draw them over the frozen snow, for the poor people who live in that cold and barren country.

Here is a representation of the way in which the Laplanders use the skins of their reindeer, in making clothes. You have before you the picture of a Lap-

VOL. X.—5

"The Children's Magazine" gave accounts of travel in various countries and poems of a moralistic nature, May 1, 1838.

OLIVER OPTIC'S MAGAZINE

OUR BOYS AND GIRLS

EVERY WEEK.

SATURDAY, APRIL 11, 1868.

Vol. III. | No. 67.

Price 6 Cents.

CONTENTS.

BOSTON:
LEE & SHEPARD.

Oliver Optic not only had his name attached to a plethora of books, but also produced the weekly periodical, "Our Boys and Girls." Boston: Lee and Shepard, 1868. (7″ by 10″).

In a supplement to "Harper's Young People," May 21, 1889, children in school are shown using both slate and paper to practice penmanship. Engraved by Ch. Baude, after a painting by Geoffroy in the Paris Exposition.

This tradition of books "just for fun" was carried over to all forms of reading matter for children, from magazines to the painting and drawing publications popular at the end of the 19th century. Although other traditionalists, as "The Children's Magazine," of the 1830's through the 1850's, retained the didactic and moralistic approach to learning, it was the magazines with a touch of humor or fun that attracted a child's eye. "Our Young Folks" was a magazine of the 1860's that presented stories, plays, poems, music, crafts, riddles, and puzzles in profusion. Later the Harper and Century publications arrived on the scene with such childhood favorites as "St. Nicholas" and "Harper's Young People." Century's "St. Nicholas" was printed monthly and the "Young People" was published weekly, but they both were offered in a bound edition containing all the issues of the year.

These magazine are not only important as examples of what children were occupying themselves with in the latter 19th century, but also because the publications served as a launching pad for many well-known artists and writers of the day. Editions of "St. Nicholas" in the 1880's often contained illustrations by Palmer Cox, Frederick Remington, R.B. Birch, F.S. Church, E.W. Kemble and other collector's favorites. It is probable that such magazines helped many struggling artists to survive in the big city of New York. Without that support, many would have returned to anonymity. The "Young People's" Post Office Box and the "St. Nicholas" Letter Box gave children a chance to let the magazines know what was of interest to them. The riddle pages were undoubtedly enjoyed again and again.

There is no doubt that books had entered the world of entertainment, for

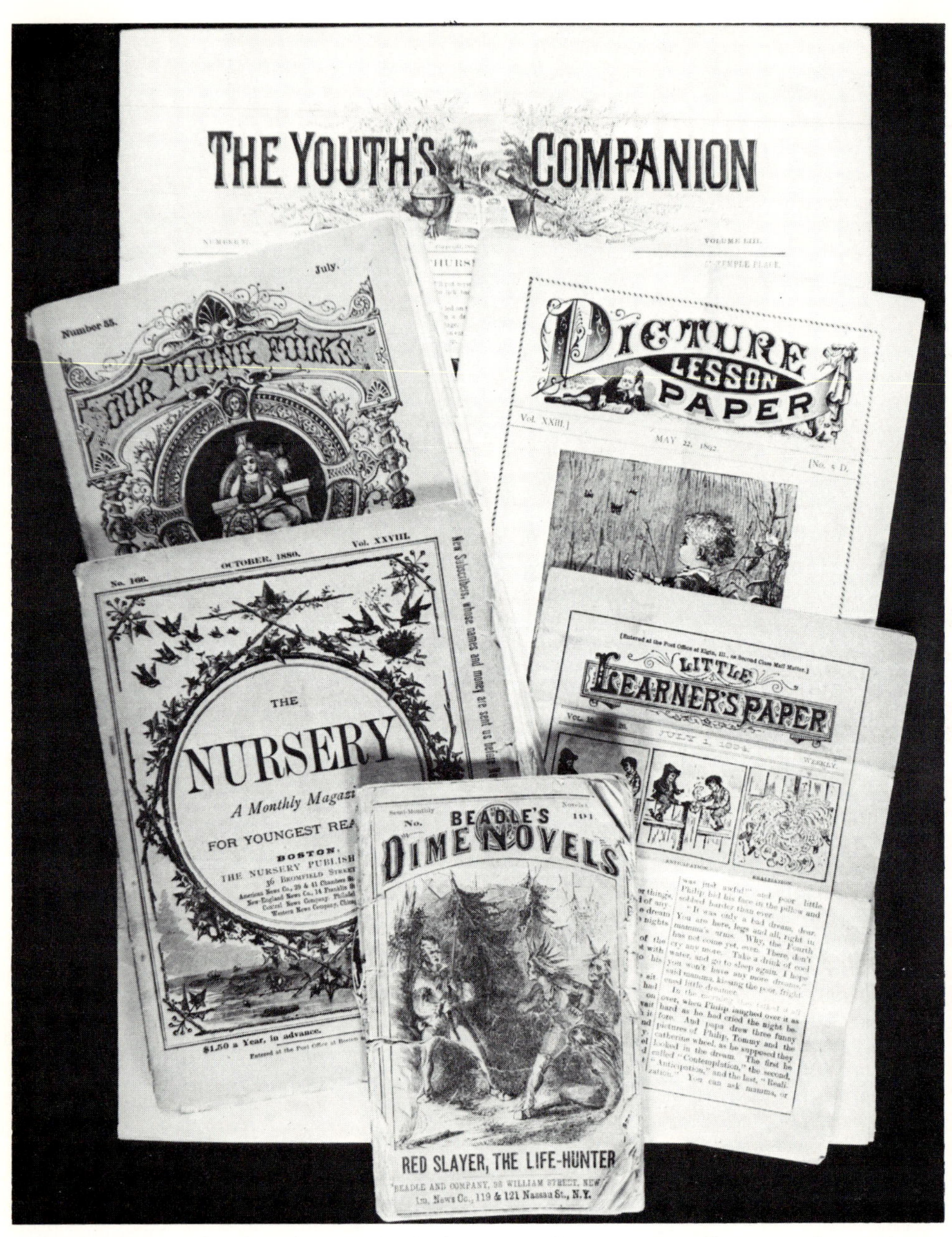

An accumulation of children's periodicals forms a collection in itself, ranging from Sunday school lesson papers to the enduring dime novel.

certainly they helped to pass many a lonely night or served as an escape for many a child. It is best to remember that many homes were secluded in the 19th century, so we find repeated references in children's books of families providing their own entertainment. A verse from a chapbook entitled, "Sports for All Seasons" aptly describes a typical evening at home in the 1830's:

"December cold, with frost and snow,
The last month of the year,
Has little to enliven us
Except his Christmas cheer—
His game of forfeits-blind man's buff—
Or other gambols gay
With many lightsome sports, to pass
The dreary nights away."

And so, books also offered ways of providing one's own fun. Softbound pamphlets and hardback editions of parlor plays were popular, as well as books such as Wilson's Book of Recitations and Dialogues," printed in 1868. Many of the recitations in this edition refer to the Civil War, indicating that once the war was over, readers enjoyed reliving important battles and heroic moments.

"The Sports for All Seasons," printed by T.W. Strong, also was a book that included illustrations and descriptions of children's toys and games. Verses and text explained the hows and whys of the hoop, the May Pole, bathing, making hay, the sportsman, and blind man's buff. Jacob Abbott, who authored the Rollo books, wrote a series entitled, "John Gay, or, Work for Boys" and "Mary Gay, or Work for Girls" circa the 1860's that offered children an explanation of occupations, just in case the fun and games ran out.

Many times, when a book is an immediate success, the story or illustrations are copied and readapted to other editions. Such was the case with "The Butterfly's Ball," which was first written by William Roscoe in 1807 for the printer J. Harris. The engravings were after drawings by William Mulready and caused an outpouring of books of a similar nature. It was the woodcuts of the butterflies and grasshoppers that struck an appealing vein and what "nonsense" it was for them to be having adventures! Besides Mrs. Dorset's "The Peacock at Home" which was printed as a sequel to the poem, almost every author was adapting insects, birds, or small animals to the role of adventure teller.

"The Royal Eagle's Feast and Ball—By Jenny Wren Who Saw It All," was an

HARPER'S

YOUNG PEOPLE

AN ILLUSTRATED WEEKLY.

VOL. X.—NO. 488 | PUBLISHED BY HARPER & BROTHERS, NEW YORK. | PRICE FIVE CENTS.

TUESDAY, MARCH 5, 1889. | Copyright, 1889, by HARPER & BROTHERS. All Rights Reserved. | $2.00 PER YEAR, IN ADVANCE.

YOUNG GERMANY.—FROM THE PAINTING BY KARL HERTEL.

The front page of "Harper's Young People" for March 5, 1889 shows an illustration of a German schoolroom, from a painting by Karl Hertel.

obvious 1810 imitation, and such verse was still a popular writing technique by the mid-19th century. McLoughlin Brothers offered "Little Frog's Lecture and Other Tales," "Wedding of Cock Robin," and "Life and Death of Jenny Wren" in their circa 1850's series. Other softbound books published about the same time, which continued the search for more nonsense, were McLoughlin's printings of "Comic Crumbs to Feed Little Ones," "Funny Pictures, Food and Fingers," and "Funny Physic and Funny Pictures."

The theme instigated by "The Butterfly's Ball" was carried quite late into the 19th century, with colorful publications such as "Buttercup's Visit to Little Stay-at-Home" in 1880 that replaced the insects with flowers. (Who knows, perhaps Loie Fuller, who performed her famous butterfly dance at the Paris Exhibition of 1900, was influenced by the influx of related stories she had read as a child.)

Two other early books deserve mention as trend setters, Heinrich Hoffman's 1848 edition of "The English Struwwelpeter; or Pretty Stories and Funny Pictures for Little Children" and S. Grimaldi's 1821 movable book, "The Toilet." Hoffman's contribution to nonsense verse included such striking figures as Shock-headed Peter who warned children, to an extreme, of the pitfalls of sloppiness. Grimaldi's hand-colored plates featured movable parts, with flaps that opened to reveal phrases. For instance, a closed jar of "fine lip salve" that revealed the word cheerfulness when the flap was lifted.

Movable books opened the door for a variety of mechanical devices, as the panoramic, diorama, pantomime, stage, paper doll, and metamorphic toybooks. These were indeed toys and functioned as both a means for play acting and entertainment. The publisher, Dean and Son of London, was one of the first mass producers of mechanical books, beginning in the 1840's. Perhaps the best seller of the line was "Dean's Moveable A.B.C." which was printed throughout the 1850's and 1860's. The movable action was achieved by pulling tabs, causing animals and figures to change their appearance.

The action books really caught on in the 1870's, with Milton Bradley and McLoughlin heading the list of American producers. The panorama, which both companies produced, consisted of a box with an open space that revealed

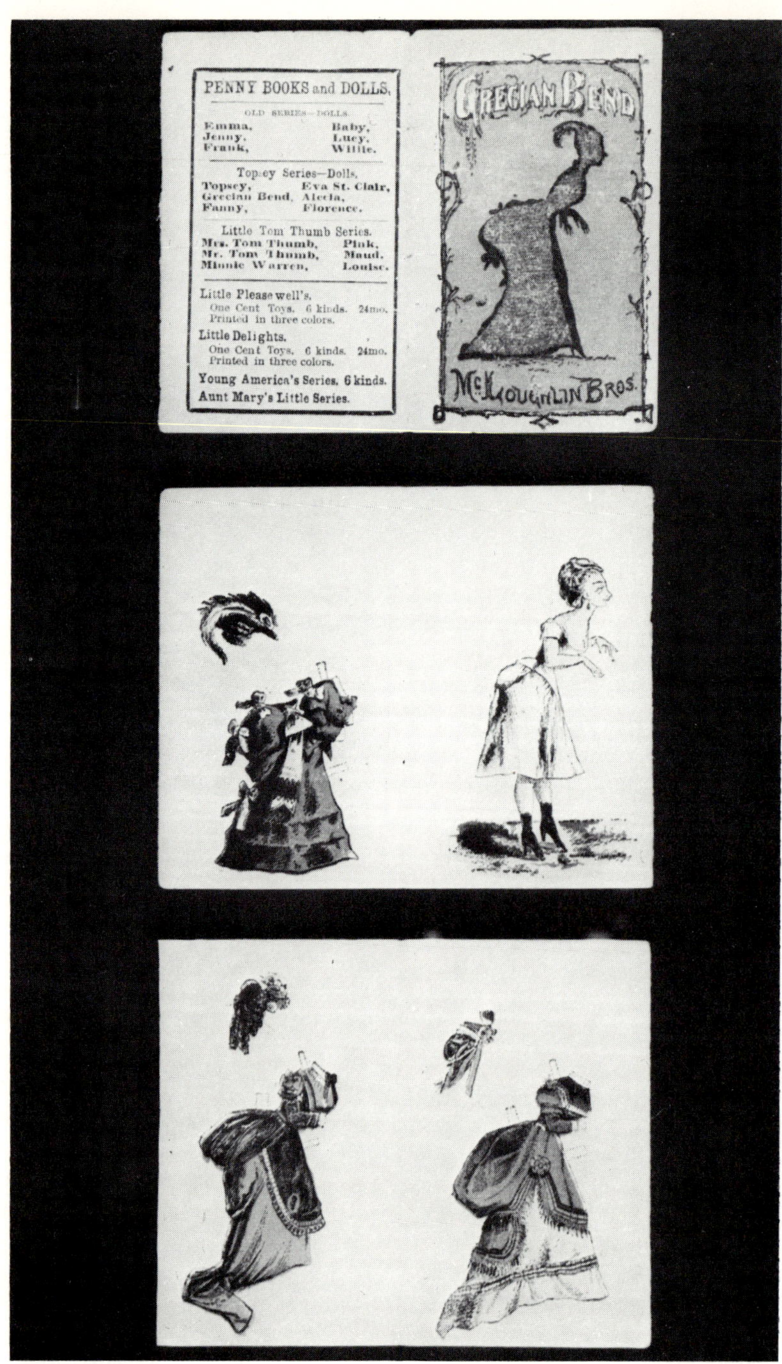

"The Grecian Bend" was a penny paper doll toybook that poked fun at one of the new fashion styles, circa 1870, McLoughlin Bros., New York. (2″ by 3″).

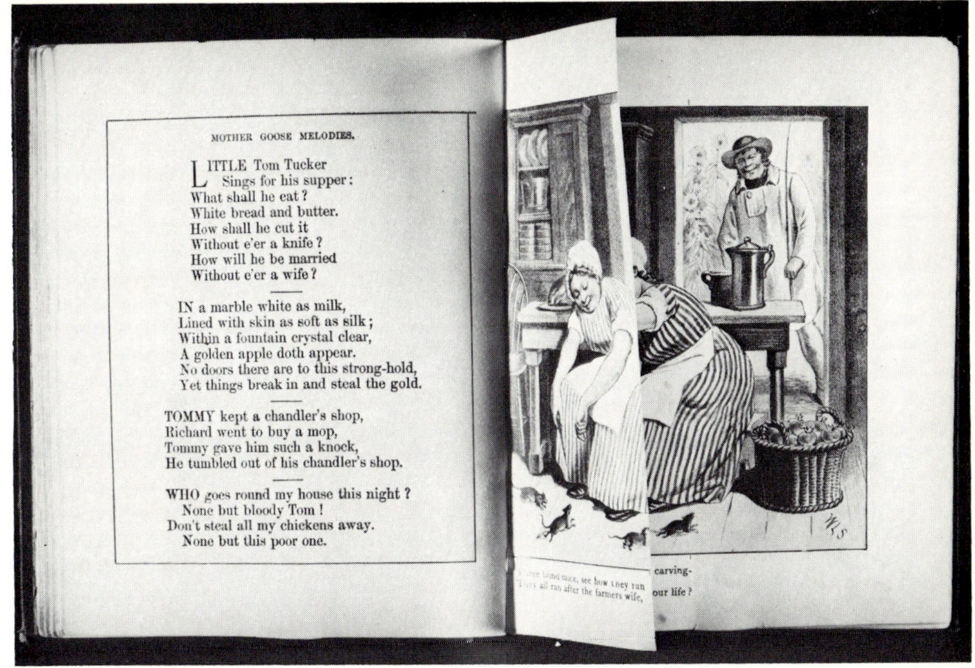

MOTHER GOOSE MELODIES.

LITTLE Tom Tucker
Sings for his supper:
What shall he eat?
White bread and butter.
How shall he cut it
Without e'er a knife?
How will he be married
Without e'er a wife?

IN a marble white as milk,
Lined with skin as soft as silk;
Within a fountain crystal clear,
A golden apple doth appear.
No doors there are to this strong-hold,
Yet things break in and steal the gold.

TOMMY kept a chandler's shop,
Richard went to buy a mop,
Tommy gave him such a knock,
He tumbled out of his chandler's shop.

WHO goes round my house this night?
None but bloody Tom!
Don't steal all my chickens away.
None but this poor one.

The technique of metamorphic or transformation pictures was applied to an 1879 edition of "Mother Goose Melodies." When the double-sized pages were flipped, the scenes changed.

an illustrated story when a crank was turned. The hand operated crank was attached to a roll of chromolithographed or hand-colored pictures, which in turn, presented such events as the "Myriopticon," a Civil War panorama, and the "Historiscope," a panorama of American history. McLoughlin also published a series of Pantomime Toybooks around the 1880's that featured text of a story plus a colorful centerfold of a stage setting. When small pages within the stage setting were flipped, the story was unfolded. The device of flipping divided pages can be traced to the Harlequinades produced in the late 18th century in England. Pictures could be turned up or turned down to form a variety of combinations. The largest manufacture of movable books towards the end of the 19th century was Lothar Meggendorfer of Germany, who favored protruding tabs to cause the action.

Another unique device applied to children's books was that of the metamorphic illustrations, or changing scenes. This technique was used in an 1879 edition of "The Old Fashioned Mother Goose Melodies, Complete with Magic Colored Pictures." Each illustration had a flap that covered half of a page, so that when the small page was lifted, the change in form was shown.

Paper dolls were also published in book form throughout the 19th century and, of course, are still fairly popular today. "The History of Little Fanny," printed in 1810 by S. & J. Fuller, was one of the first toybooks accompanied by a series of hand-colored figures and costumes.

"The Educated Pig" songster told of a learned hog who could, ". . . add, subtract and knows the rules, as well as any boy at school." Lancaster, Pennsylvania, 1873. (4″ by 6¼″).

Each set contained seven aquatinted cut-out figures, four hats, an interchangeable head that fitted in a slot in the body, and a story book. After 1857, McLoughlin Brothers issued paper dolls to accompany contemporary nursery stories as "Goody Two-Shoes" and "Little Red Riding Hood," and also celebrities as Tom Thumb and Commodore Nutt of Barnum circus fame.

It is interesting that so many well-known authors and artists dabbled in books just for fun. Charles Dodgson, the actual name of Lewis Carroll, epitomized the movement for enjoyable children's matter, in his 1876 "The Hunting of the Snark." Kate Greenaway brought her unmistakeable illustrative style to pasttime books as "The Little Folks Painting Book" of 1879 and an 1889 edition of "Kate Greenaway's Book of Games." Certainly bibliophily, the love of books for their own sake, aptly applies to the collecting of children's riddle, limerick, movable and game books.

Related Books and Current Values

"The History of Little Fanny," 4th edition, London: printed for S. and J. Fuller, 15 pages, 1810, seven aquatinted paper doll figures, a movable head and four head pieces, in a printed slipcase, value $125.

"Rural Amusements," Mary Eliot, 6 mo., William Darton, 1820, colored plates, half morocco, value $95.

"Comical Creatures with Laughable Features," Thomas Nelson and Sons, London, Edinburgh, and New York, 2nd series, Sixpenny Picture Books, color illustrations, pictorial covers, 1877, value $22.

"Wedding of Cock Robin," Pleasure Books for Children, McLoughlin Brothers, 24 Beekman St., N.Y., softbound, hand-colored illustrations, circa 1850's, value $30.

"Kate Greenaway's Book of Games," 24 full-page color illustrations by Kate Greenaway, engraved and printed by Edmund Evans, London: George Routledge, board cover, (n.d.) 1889, value $100.

"The Little Folks Painting Book," 107 outline engravings for watercolor painting by Kate Greenaway, with verses and stories by George Weatherly, London: Cassell, Petter, Gilpin, (n.d.) 1879, value $125.

"Comical Rhymes of Ancient Times, Dug up into Jokes for Small Folks," published by Hurd and Houghton, 459 Broome St., N.Y., printed in red and black inks, softbound, circa 1870, value $12.

"Life and Death of Cock Robin," Mark's Toy Books, published by Fisk & Little, 82 State St., Albany, N.Y., softbound, hand-colored illustrations, circa late 1840's, value $30.

"The Children's Holiday Coach," London: Ernest Nister, E.P. Dutton & Co., New York, a three-dimensional standup, illustrated with a poem, enclosed in an illustrated envelope, 1895, value $50.

"The Paignon," F.C. Westley, twelve lithographed plates with 30 of 65 figures to be fitted into slots in the plates, hand-colored, board covers, gilt label, circa 1830, value $230.

"The History and Adventures of Little Henry," S. & J. Fuller, head and seven acquatinted figures (lacks hats), printed green wrappers and slip-case, 16 mo, 1810, value $85.

"A Book of Nonsense," by Edward Lear, Frederick Warne & Co., New York: Scribner, Welford, and Co., illustrated, 1870, value $40.

"Funny Pictures, Food and Fingers," Aunt Oddamadodd's Series, McLoughlin Brothers, 24 Beekman St., New York, softbound, illustrated, circa 1850's, value $20.

"The Butterfly's Ball," William Roscoe, hand-colored engravings, original wrappers with colored label, William Belch, circa 1822, value $110.

"The Peacock at Home and Other Poems," by Catherine Anne Dorset, Grant & Griffith, hand-colored illustrations by William Mulready, original wrappers, 1844, value $75.

"Alice's Adventures in Wonderland," by Lewis Carroll, Macmillan & Co., New York, with 42 illustrations by John Tenniel, 1st published American edition, 1866, red cloth, value $800.

"Bluebeard," Pantomime Books, McLoughlin Bros., N.Y., color illustrated board covers and contents, small flip pages within a stage setting, circa 1880's, value $22.

"Baby's Lullaby Book," Charles Stuart Pratt, L. Prang and Co., Boston, colored illustrations, circa 1890's, value $25.

"Music Made Easy," hand-colored illustrations, original wrappers, circa 1845, value $175.

"Moveable Alphabet Book," published by Dean & Son, London, hand-colored illustrations, pull tabs, figures move, 1863, value $55.

"A Rare Cat," 9 inches by 11½ inches, Chromolithographed pop-up book, four-layer scene with text, heavy board cover, no publisher, circa 1870's value $35.

"Cinderella," London, Dean & Son, five sets and nine chromolithographed changes, overlapping illustrations, Pantomime Toy Books, No. 3, circa 1880's, value $50.

"The Butterfly's Ball, and the Grasshopper's Feast," by William Roscoe, printed for J. Harris, London, corner of St. Paul's Church Yard, engraved after drawings by William Mulready, original boards, 12 mo, Jany 1st 1807, value $360.

"Magic Mother Goose Melodies, Complete with Magic Colored Pictures," G.W. Carleton & Co. publisher, Donaldson Brothers designer and printer, metamorphic bi-colored illustrations, overlapping flip pages, 1879, value $40.

"The Lady's Toilet," Rock Brothers and Payne, nine improving prints with flaps and descriptive verses, (lacks one flap), circa 1855, value $100.

"Rummical Rhymes with Pictures to Match," published by Hurd and Houghton, 459 Broome St., New York, softbound, red and black printing, circa 1870's, value $10.

"The Bad Child's Book of Beasts," by Hilaire Belloc, verses by H.B., pictures by Lord Basil Blackwood, Oxford: Alden & Co. Ltd., Bocardo Press, 35, Cornmarket St., London: Simpkin, Marshall, Hamilton, Kent, and Co. Ltd., 1896, value $25.

"Puss in Boots," Pantomime Books, McLoughlin Bros., N.Y., color illus. board covers and contents, small flip pages within a stage setting, circa 1880's, value $18.

"Riddle Book, Aunt Fanny's Fairy Tales," Pleasure Books, McLoughlin Brothers, 24 Beekman St., New York, softbound, hand-colored illustrations, illuminated covers, circa 1850's, value $25.

"Buttercups Visit to Little Stay-at-Home," by L. Clarkson, New York: E.P. Dutton & Company, color illustrations by author, board covers, 1881, value $17.50.

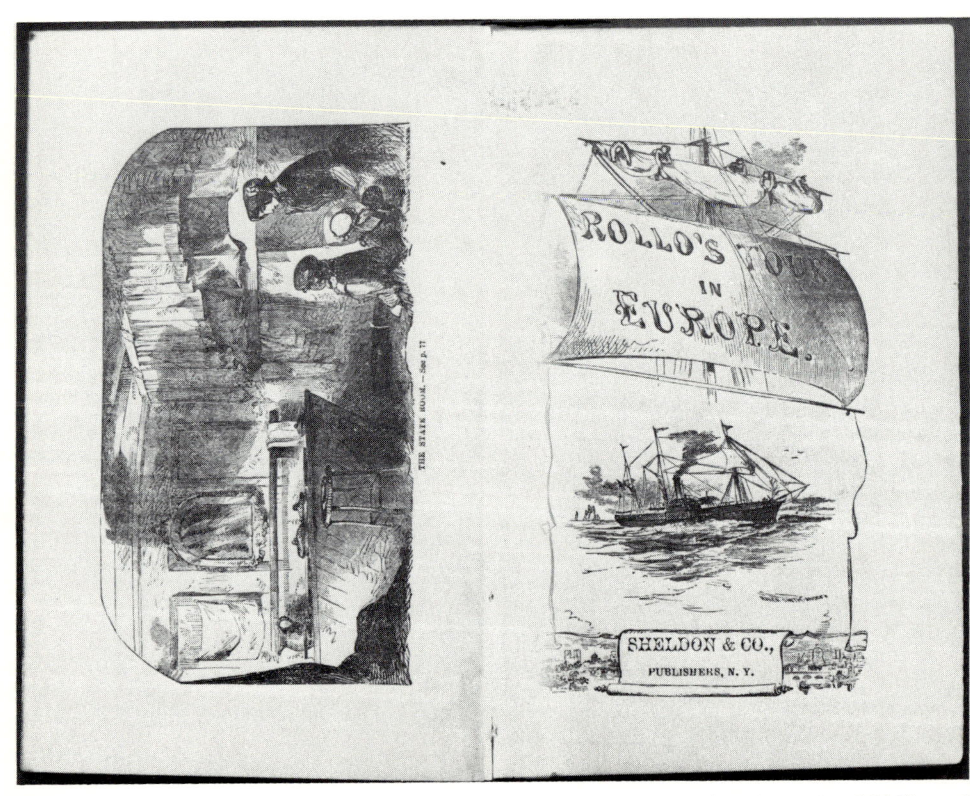

Jacob Abbott's adventures of the boy, Rollo, spanned at least a decade in the 1840's and 1850's and took him to many different countries.

Chapter 7

People, Places, and Events

"Can rhetorician or logician
Describe with aught that's like precision
The rapture that dilates his soul,
Now his own master, and beyond control?
His fancy soars aloft, like a skyrocket!
Where shall he go?
He doesn't know,
Although "the world's before him where to choose,"
And he's got on a bran' new pair of shoes,
And two bright shilings in his trousers' pocket."

– From Cruikshank's Comic Almanac for 1836.

The fellow mentioned in the previous verse might well have spent his shillings if he had purchased a book and saved wear and tear on his new pair of shoes. For the element of nonfiction brought distant lands, celebrities, and important occasions into the reach of every child or adult by simply turning a page.

Whereas the geography books offered facts of an instructional nature, they could not compare in interest to the exciting and adventuresome tales of the far West. Likewise, children could travel by way of the printed page or colorful illustration to most any place of their choosing, rather than being restricted to a teacher's choice of local history. Granted, many of the Rocky Mountain adventure stories and Rollo's tours around the world were not nonfiction by any means, but it was the ingredient of truth or basic facts that attracted children to these series of books.

In a bound copy of "The Children's Magazine" for 1838, children were given text discussing the statues of Thebes, a church in Venice, a New England prayer, and traveling in Lapland. Occasional illustrations gave credence to the stories and increased a child's awareness, even though a camel in the accompanying Thebes illustration appears to be a sea monster. It is interesting that this small volume has an early bookplate from a Sunday school library fastened inside the front cover, indicating that churches encouraged children to read about faraway places, particularly if the publication retained a religious and moralistic outlook.

One of the first to tempt children to reach out to other parts of the world was Isaac Taylor. In 1821 the London writer authored "Scenes in America, for the Little Tarry-At-Home Travellers" and continued to write books about various exciting places. He obviously felt that any child was not destined to remain a tarry-at-home and through books had no excuses for living in a secluded shell. Besides his excellent geographies, Samuel G. Goodrich (1793–1860) wrote a number of books regarding important figures of history, as his 1829 edition of "Stories About Captain John Smith for the Instruction & Amusement of Children."

The continuous narrative, particularly regarding a series of adventures of a hero who was readily identified by past exploits, was an immediate hit with the younger generation. In the preface to one of Jacob Abbott's (1803–1879) Rollo books, he recounts that, "The books are intended to be books of instruction rather than of mere amusement, and in perusing them, the reader may feel assured that all the information which they contain, not only in respect to the countries visited, and to the customs, usages, and modes of life that are described, but also in regard to the general character of the incidents and adventures that the young travellers meet with, is in most strict accordance with fact."

Abbott's stories revolved around Rollo, a boy of twelve years of age, his parents Mr. and Mrs. Holiday, and various other relatives. Many tricks in text copied by later serial writers were Abbott's innovations. For instance, his technique of using names, as Mr. & Mrs. Holiday, to bring immediate images to mind and also condensing a page's context to a short phrase at the top, as "The loss of the trunk is discovered." His illustrated books were popular in the 1840's and 1850's and included, "Rollo's Corres-

Supposedly, "The African Widow" was based on an account in an English report of a society instituted for the relief of the poor Africans. Published by the American Tract Society, circa the 1850's. (3″ by 4½″).

pondence" (1841), "Rollo at School" (1849), and "Rollo's Tour in Europe" (1853), among others. Despite Abbott's claims of his books being mainly of an instructional nature, his stories were amusing and calculated to appeal to children as well as to an adult reading the tales to a child.

Other books carried a message of truth in disguise, as Harriet Beecher Stowe's immortal, "Uncle Tom's Cabin." This novel at first appeared in the "National Era" magazine as a serial in 1851–1852. Its anti-slavery theme was digested by parents and children alike. The "Slave's Friend," a periodical of only 2¼″ x 3½″ in size, was specifically printed for children in the 1840's. A typical issue displayed a woodcut of two "stolen children" who were brought in the brig "America" from Africa. A poem entitled "The Poor Mother" pleads with the readers and states, "Help! oh, help! Thou God of Christians! Save a mother from despair; Cruel whitemen steal my children. God of Christians! Hear my prayer." Children were further advised to put " . . . money you earn into the Anti-Slavery treasury . . . Thus the people can be taught how wicked a thing slavery is." It was the children who read these tiny volumes that would grow up to fight for the same causes in the Civil War.

Around the mid-part of the 19th century, a tremendous market of books

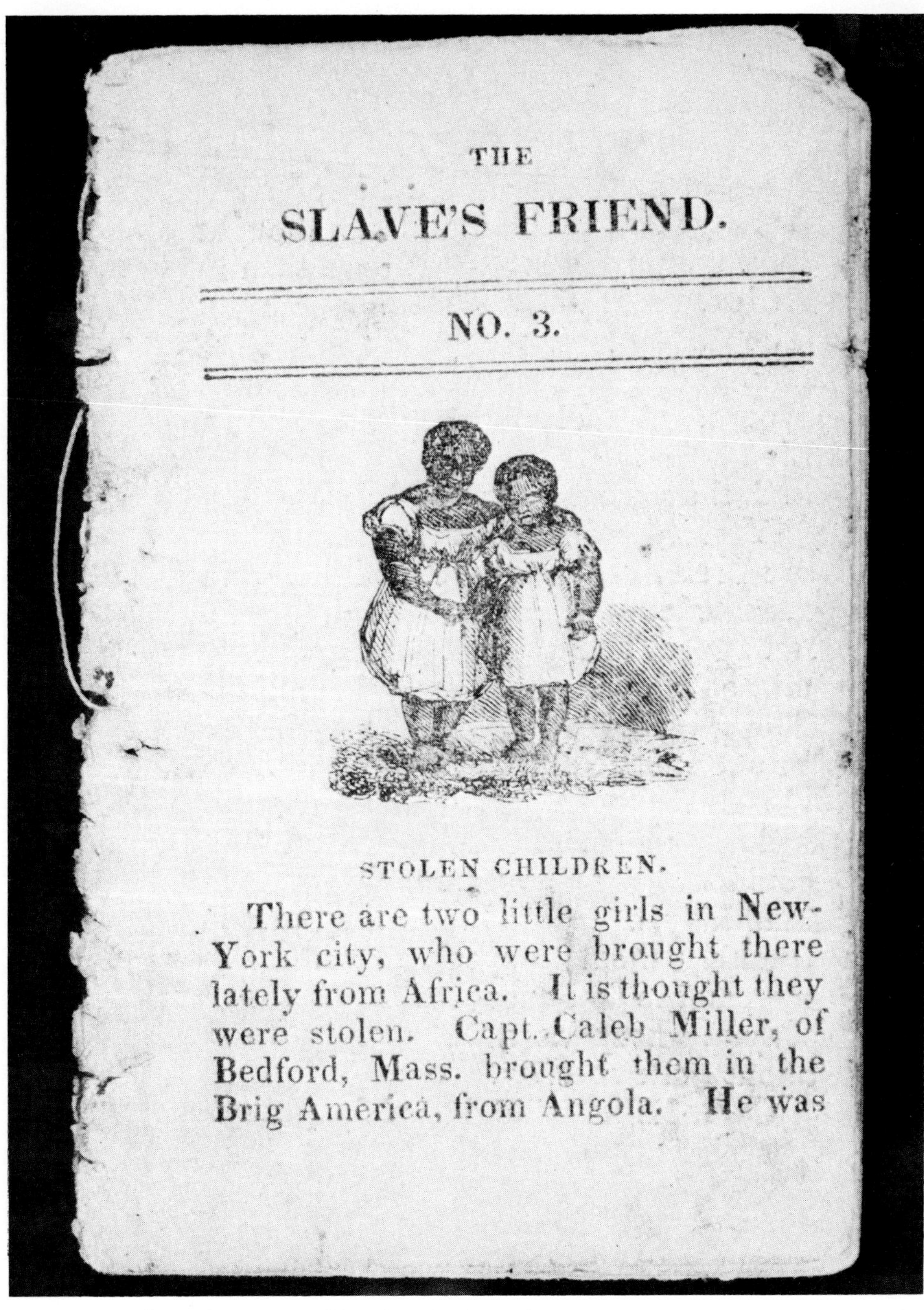
THE

SLAVE'S FRIEND.

NO. 3.

STOLEN CHILDREN.

There are two little girls in New-York city, who were brought there lately from Africa. It is thought they were stolen. Capt. Caleb Miller, of Bedford, Mass. brought them in the Brig America, from Angola. He was

A periodical of chapbook size, "The Slave's Friend," told children about slavery atrocities. Circa 1840, woodcut illustration. (2½" by 4").

ADVENTURES

OF A

PIONEER BOY,

While a Prisoner of War.

ALVAN Q. BACON,

HIS CAPTURE AT THE BATTLE OF SHILOH AND ESCAPE FROM MACON, GA., GOING SIXTY MILES IN CANOES BY NIGHT, GOT TO A UNION GUNBOAT, AND SAILED BY OCEAN TO NEW YORK.

WRITTEN BY HIMSELF.

Sold for the Benefit of his Father, who is nearly Blind.

Price, 15 Cents.

True stories based on the Civil War fascinated youth, such as this chapbook, "Adventures of a Pioneer Boy, While a Prisoner of War." By Q. Bacon, circa 1866. (5½″ by 8¼″).

The Sailor Boy.

Though the strained mast should quiver as a reed,
And the rent canvas fluttering strew the gale,
Still must I on. . . . . . BYRON.

SHIPWRECKS

AND

DISASTERS AT SEA.

THE RAFT.

BOSTON:

PRINTED AND PUBLISHED BY S. N. DICKINSON,
52 Washington Street.

1837.

Certainly, one of the subjects that appealed to boys was the sea, as noted in this 1837 edition of "Shipwrecks and Disasters at Sea." Boston: S.N. Dickinson.

appeared that were aimed to appeal to young boys. The sea voyage, shipwreck, and pirate books of the 1830's and 1840's had been avidly read by young gentlemen; but now a new pastime arose, that of reading sporting novels. R.S. Surtees (1803–1864) authored a series of these novels issued in monthly supplements in the 1850's that frequently featured hand-colored illustrations by John Leech. Surtees pictorial and gilt adorned bindings, which were available at the end of the year, were treasured by youngsters in printings covering over thirty years, as seen on his 1853 edition of "Mr. Sponge's Sporting Tour."

In the 1860's, children could read about the adventures of Oliver Optic either in book form, or in "Oliver Optic's Magazine," which was published weekly. Titles as "Adventures in the Wilderness" (1869) and "The Boy Makes the Man" (1873) were typical of books by other authors that followed, as well as Sage's "Rocky Mountain Life or Startling Scenes and Perilous Adventures in the Far West" that was reprinted innumerable times in the 1880's. Robert M. Ballantyne (1825–1894) wrote more than 100 boys' adventure tales starting with "Hudson's Bay" in 1848. G.A. Henty (1832–1902) was equally prolific with

This trade card was used to promote one of Oliver Optic's charming books, "Our Little Ones." It was priced at $1.50 for a hardbound edition, Boston, circa 1880.

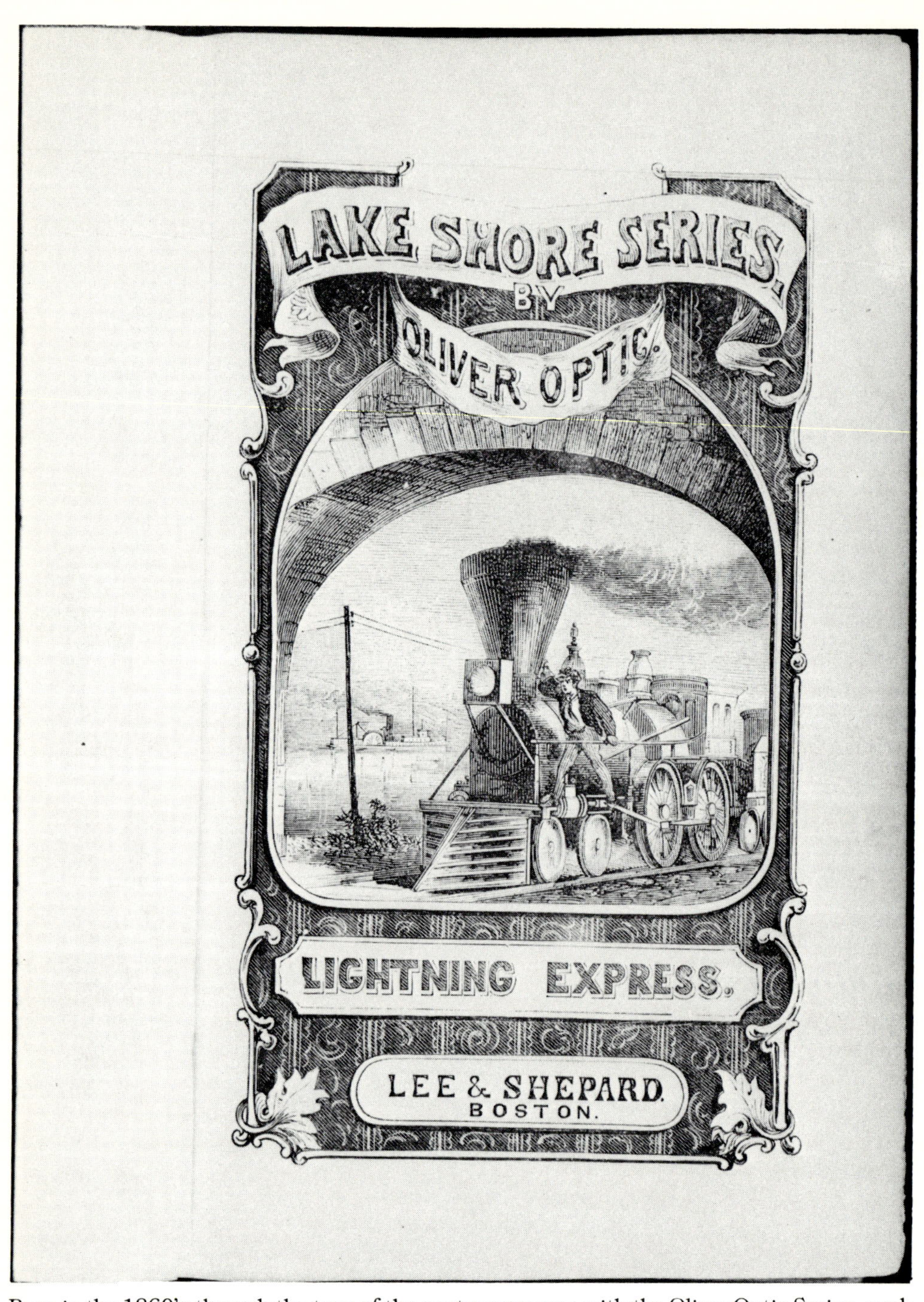

Boys in the 1860's through the turn of the century grew up with the Oliver Optic Series, such as the "Lightning Express," printed by Lee & Shepard of Boston, 1870. (4″ by 7″).

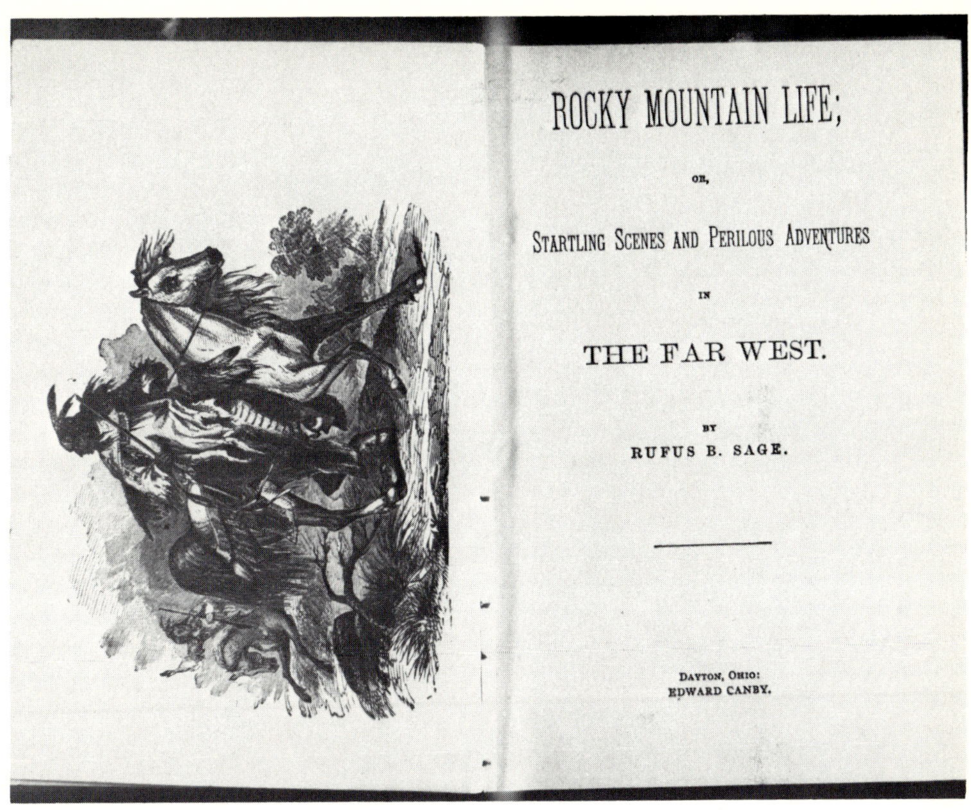
ROCKY MOUNTAIN LIFE;

OR,

STARTLING SCENES AND PERILOUS ADVENTURES

IN

THE FAR WEST.

BY

RUFUS B. SAGE.

DAYTON, OHIO:
EDWARD CANBY.

The majority of children's books in the latter part of the 19th century were slanted towards subjects appealing to boys, as tales of adventure, sports, and the Far West.

such tales as "Bonnie Prince Charlie" (1888) and "By Right of Conquest: or With Cortez in Mexico" (1891). Not to be forgotten are the Horatio Alger classics, as "Ragged Dick" (1868) and "Rufus & Rose" (1870). Truly the boys in this era were expected to be the main reading audience, for the publications aimed at girls were in a much lighter vein, with frivolous accounts of craftmaking, poetry, and fashion news.

A pilot on a Mississippi River steamer by the name of Samuel L. Clemens (1835–1910) brought humor to the adventure tale. His pseudonym, Mark Twain, was taken from the leadsman's call and became a familiar associate to the portrayal of youth, river life, and romantic sentimentality. The 1876 printing of "Tom Sawyer" and his 1884 edition of "Huckleberry Finn" are classic representations of American life in the 19th century. A British author who gained equal recognition was Rudyard Kipling (1865–1936) with stories of India and children's books as "The Jungle Book" (1894).

Important events of the day were brought into a child's world by way of periodicals and books specifically dealing with an occasion. Many publishers printed Centennial series in honor of the exhibition of 1876, which was held in

The initials of the pseudonym of Samuel Clemens became identifiable by children and adults alike. The frontispiece to the 1890 edition of "Sketches by Mark Twain" bore an illustration of some of his characterizations.

"St. Nicholas Magazine" was one of the first children's publications to utilize the photographic process. "St. Nicholas," 1891.

Philadelphia. Such a book was the "Young Folks' Centennial Rhymes" that contained verses and plays dealing with American history by the writer Will Carlton. Mr. Carlton explains in the preface that he offers the rhymes, ". . . in plain words, but without descending to baby talk." The lovable character, Samantha, who traveled through a series of adventures in the 1870's and 1880's, also visited the 1876 exhibition in "Josiah Allen's Wife as a P.A. and P.I., or Samantha at the Centennial." Other event editions that were written at a level for young adults were "The Queen's Resolve—I Will Be Good," a Jubilee Memorial of 1886 in honor of Queen Victoria, and "The Christmas Bower" of 1892 that contained chromolithographs of the Columbian Exposition interspersed in the book.

Whereas boys were seeking adventure in their reading, the proper, but curious, Victorian girls learned much about the arts, travel, and fashion. Louisa May Alcott (1832—1888) was one of the few writers in the latter part of the 19th century who decided to gain the young girls back into the folds of reading novels, and headed her series of books with "Little Women" in 1868. But the majority of reading matter for girls consisted of periodical mainstays as "St. Nicholas," and

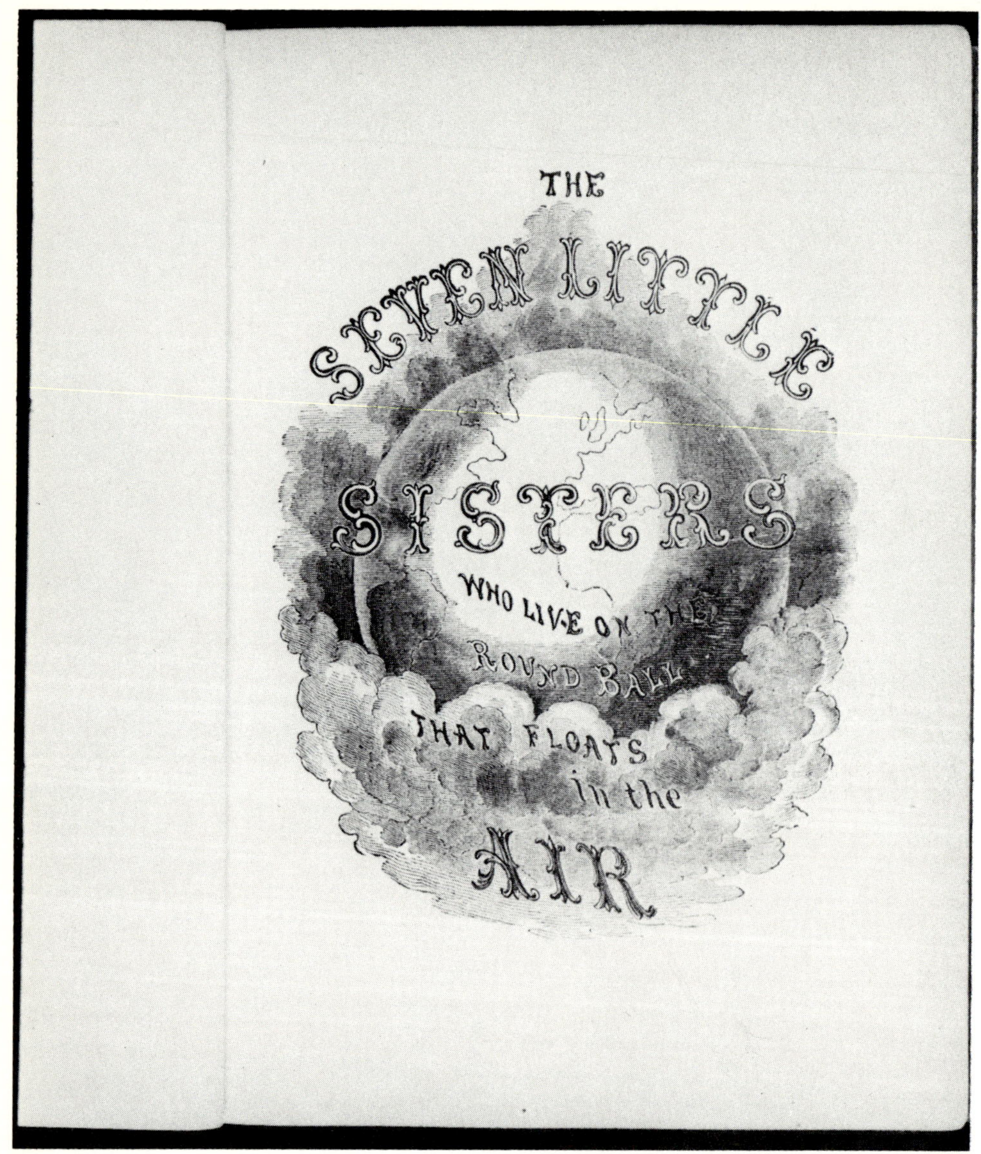

Besides having a unique title, "The Seven Little Sisters Who Live on the Ball that Floats in the Air," was noted for the facts describing the various races of man, their modes of life and action. One of a series by Jane Andrews, Boston, 1869.

even Louisa May Alcott contributed stories to such publications. Other magazines, that were usually hardbound at the end of the year, offered crocheting instructions, painting directions, dress designs, new crafts, travel stories, children's poems, and puzzle pages that appealed mainly to girls.

It is obvious that such Victorian publications were molding young girls into proper housewives and interesting conversationalists. Female pastimes were limited to the household, whereas boys were invited, by way of the book, to seek adventures around the world.

Related Books and Current Values

"Chatterbox for 1887," Estes & Lauriat, Boston, Massachusetts, illuminated board covers, numerous illustrations, 1887, value $15.

"Young Folks' Centennial Rhymes," by Will Carlton, Harper & Brothers, Publishers, Franklin Square, New York, illustrated, cloth bound, 1876, value $7.50.

"Who was the First Architect?," Ninepenny Books, The Busy-Bee Series, Thomas Nelson and Sons, London, Edinburgh, and New York, colored frontispiece, illuminated sides, engravings, cloth, 16 mo., 1877, value $15.

"The Boys of 1812," by Prof. J. Russell Soley, Estes & Lauriat, Boston, Massachusetts, illustrated, cloth, quarto, 1887, value $20.

"Shooting on the Wing,—a Book for Young Sportsmen," by an Old Gamekeeper, The Handicraft Publication Company, 37 Park Row, New York, illustrated, green cloth with gilt, eight pages of sporting advertisements in the back, 1873, value $25.

"The Christmas Wreath," London: T. Nelson and Sons, Edinburgh and New York, pictorial boards, color illustrations, 1877, value $10.

"Great Grandmother's Girls in New France," by Lizzie W. Champney, Estes & Lauriat, Boston, Massachusetts, cloth, gilt, 1887, value $6.

"Adventures of Famous Travellers in Many Lands," New York: Wm. L. Allison, 93 Chamber and 75 Reade Streets, Arundel Edition, illustrated, circa 1880's, value $15.

"Milkanwatha," by Marc Anthony Henderson, third edition, published by D.R. Niver, Albany, New York, illustrated by Frank Beard, cloth, 16 mo, 1883, value $18.

"Zigzag Journeys in India," published by Estes & Lauriat, Boston, Massachusetts, illustrated, illuminated board covers, small quarto, 1887, value $7.

"Shipwrecks and Disasters at Sea," Boston: printed and published by S.N. Dickinson, 52 Washington St., 100 engravings, 1837, value $35.

"The Bear-Worshipers," by Edward Greey, Lee and Shepard Publishers, 47 Franklin St., Boston, illustrated, boards, 1883, value $15.

"Little Ones Annual," edited by William T. Adams, (Oliver Optic), Estes & Lauriat, Boston, illustrated, board covers, 1887, value $18.

"Young Benjamin Franklin, or, The Right Road Through Life," by Henry Mayhew, Harper & Brothers, New York, illustrated by John Gilbert, cloth, 16 mo, 1876, value $12.

"The Swanee River," by Stephen Collins Foster, published by Ticknor & Co., Boston, pictorial cloth cover, illustrated, 1887, value $18.

"Mark Twain's Sketches New and Old," (Samuel L. Clemens), The American Publishing Co., Hartford, Connecticut, and Chicago, Illinois, blue and gilt cloth, illustrated, 1890, value $20.

"The Queen's Resolve—I Will Be Good," by the Rev. Charles Bullock B.D., London: Home Words Office, 7 Paternoster Square, E.C., A Jubilee Memorial, engravings, red cloth with gilt, pictorial cover, 1886, value $12.50.

"Elizabeth; or, The Exiles of Siberia—A Tale from the French of Madame Cottin," Nimmo's one shilling illustrated juvenile books, London and Edinburgh, colored frontispiece, cloth, illum., 1878, value $20.

"Our Boys in China," by Harry W. French, Lee, and Shepard, publishers, 47 Franklin St., Boston, engravings, pictorial cloth, 1883, value $12.50.

"Boy's Own Book," A complete encyclopedia of Athletic, Scientific, Recreative, Outdoor and Indoor Exercises and Diversions, R. Worthington, Publisher, 770 Broadway, New York, illustrated, cloth, gilt, circa 1880, value $22.

"The Boys Book of Sports," Century Co. Publishers, New York, 300 illustrations, 1887, value $25.

"The Youth's Companion," Perry Mason & Co., 41 Temple Place, Boston, Massachusetts, bound annual edition of a weekly, illustrated, 1888, value $25.

"The Boy Makes the Man," T. Nelson and Sons, London, Edinburgh, and New York, colored frontispiece and title page, illustrated, green cloth with gilt, 1873, value $7.50.

"St. Nicholas Songs," edited by Prof. Waldo S. Pratt, Century Co. Publishers, New York, 112 songs, 140 illustrations, cloth binding, 1887, value $15.

"St. Nicholas Magazine," bound annual, Century Co. Publishers, New York, numerous illustrations, red cloth, 1889, value $12.50.

"The Children's Magazine," bound annual for 1838, containing excerpts from current publications, illustrated, marbled boards, value $18.

"Rocky Mountain Adventure, or Startling Scenes and Perilous Adventures in the Far West," by Rufus B. Sage, Dayton, Ohio: Edward Canby Publishers, illustrated, circa 1880's, value $15.

"Josiah Allen's Wife as a P.A. and P.I. or Samantha at the Centennial," Hartford, Connecticut: American Publishing Company, illustrated, green and gilt cloth, 1881, value $10.

"Baby World," edited by Mrs. Mary Mapes Dodge, Century Co., New York, 300 pages, illustrated, illum. boards, 1887, value $8.

"The Christmas Bower," Juvenile Publishing Co., red and blue cloth pictorial cover, salesman's sample, wood engravings and color plates of the Columbian Exposition, 1892, value $20.

Marbling.

A book marbler of 1872 places two dictionaries into a solution of swirling dyes, producing a marbling effect.

Chapter 8

Covers and Care

"Through and through the inspired leaves,
Ye Maggots make your windings;
But, oh, respect his lordship's taste,
And spare the golden bindings!"
—Burns

Have you ever stopped to wonder why you have become interested in collecting old children's books? We have examined several reasons for acquiring these treasures of past childhoods, from appealing illustrations to instructional text, but basically, one has to feel a certain admiration before attempting to enter into the field. Perhaps it is an admiration for the author's work or artist's style, but more than likely, one cannot quite explain to someone else the attraction for the sometimes crude and flimsy paper ephemera that another would have long ago discarded. As for children's books, they seem to take on almost human characteristics; they may become a friend to seek in times of discouragement or represent the perfect child who cannot talk back! Milton once said that " . . . Childhood shows the man, as morning shows the day." Thus, if childhood is an indication of adulthood, then children's literature can form the adult reading habits of a person, and perhaps even influence opinions in later situations of life. These small treasures have suddenly gained a great deal in importance.

So, if some of your books begin to take on humanistic qualities, it is only because they have suddenly become endearing to you. And, as a good friend, books should be treated with care and they will return benefits tenfold.

Any extremes in temperature or exposure to moisture will cause untold damage to your treasures, from slight browning spots, termed foxing, to rippled pages and sprung bindings. Likewise, care should be taken to select a proper storing place for your books. Preferably, one would like an enclosed, dust-free location with plenty of room for storage, and adjustable shelving for any size of an acquisition. Careless stacking of books can result in a book being knocked to the floor, resulting most assuredly in a cracked or loose spine.

To further the analogy, we discover that a book has a spine, a body, and an outer cover or skin. The body of the book is produced by the printer who sends the sheets on to the bindery, where they are folded by machinery and bundled by a press. The prelims, as the endpapers and title page, are folded separately, any plates are added, the contents gathered, sewn, pressed, or nipped, edges trimmed, spines glued, rounded, and backed. Automation again takes over and puts the book into the triple lining and head-band machine, where it is completed, unless edges are to be decorated.

Of course, this procedure applies only to hardbound children's books, the production of a softbound chapbook was a much simpler matter. The rough, high rag content sheet of paper was folded into eight, sixteen, or twenty-four pages and then the leaves were hand cut. Paper wrappers were usually pictorial, with an appropriate woodcut from the story, or decorated with various fancy type settings partially framing any text. The owner sometimes stitched the leaves together for increase in wear or pasted a strip of cloth along the front folds for reinforcement. The chapmen's pack carried a variety of these small toybooks, which sold for pennies and had the advantage of taking up little space.

The edge of a children's hardbound book was usually plain, but sometimes it was adorned with color, marbling, or gilt. The plain colors were applied evenly with a sponge—the marbling effect, which was also used on end papers, was a more complicated procedure.

During the 17th century, calf and sheepskin bindings were occasionally marbled in France to appear as tortoise shell, or varigated to imitate marble. The process also was applied to end papers and edges of books. At about the same time in England, marbling was used with paper covered boards of quarter-calf leather and on end papers. The end papers were made by lowering the plain sheets onto trays containing sticky size, and then side-toothed combs stirred

Left: An early color illustrated board cover with cloth spine, "Book of Recitations," 1868. Right: Cloth binding with chromolithograph attached upper left, T. Nelson, New York, circa 1870's.

patterns into the dyes previously added to the tray. Marbling was later used for boards of half and quarter-bound books in the form of Victorian bindings. The "Children's Magazine," a quarter-bound book of the 1830's through the 1850's, combined a cloth covered spine with marbled boards for its cover.

In the application of gilt, the edges were scraped and coated with a mixture of powdered black lead, egg whites, and water. The gold leaf, which is placed on a slightly greased piece of paper, is then pressed onto the book's edge until it adheres. Finally, the dried gold is polished until gleaming. Besides being decorative, the edge gilding also helps to keep out dust.

The contents of a hard cover book is "married" to the binding at the casing machine. The covers are usually made from machine-cut boards, which are glued together with pre-cut cloth, pressed, blocked, and any additional lettering added. The casing machine then forms the backbone or spine and attaches, by gluing, to the end papers. After being pressed, the completed book is frequently covered with wrappers or a dust jacket.

The art of the bookbinder has spanned hundreds of years and encompassed a variety of materials. At first vellum or calfskin seemed to be adequate, but this was soon found to be rather flimsy and easily damaged. Wooden boards were

An ornate cover of red cloth stamped with gold reveals the bookbinder's art. London, 1886, from, "The Queen's Resolve — I Will be Good."

then used, and although firm, they were bulky and tore from the spines. Finally, both were combined. The dawn of the blocking machine and the invention of movable type made mass production a real possibility and old methods were discarded. Fancy book bindings, that are so much sought after by collectors today, became too costly and time consuming. Cloth bindings and paper boards replaced leather towards the mid-part of the 19th century, with leather being reserved for special editions.

There may be some confusion as to the difference between a full, quarter, or half-type of binding. Most leather, paper, and cloth bound books are of full binding; that is to say, one piece of material covers the entire outside of the book including the spine. In a quarter binding, the spine of the book is covered with a different material than the boards, or front and reverse, of the book. This can be noted in the McGuffey readers and the majority of the Olney and Sanders geography series printed around the 1840's and 1850's. A leather spine was combined with pictorial paper covered boards. Frequently these volumes contain spine damage because the leather could not withstand constant use.

After the mid-part of the 19th century, a cloth spine was found to be somewhat more durable, and paper covered boards were still retained mainly for their cheapness and adaptation for pictorial use. McLoughlin, Raphael Tuck, and R. Worthington are just a few of the publishers who prefered quarter bindings for their series of children's books in the 1870's and 1880's, combining a cloth spine with colorful pictorial paper board covers. Another type of binding, seldom seen on children's books, is the half binding. In addition to the spine being covered with a different material, the corner pieces of the boards are augmented with a reinforcement material.

In the late 1880's into the 20th century, many new issues of books for children were peddled house to house by salespersons. The seller was given a salesman's sample of the book to be sold, which contained the most important portions of the text and the majority of the illustrations. The binding strip of the spine was attached to the inside of the front or back cover and lined pages were provided at the end of the text for the agent to keep track of his calls. Many annuals and holiday books, such as the "Christmas Bower" and "The Young American Annual" were sold in this manner during the 1890's.

To recapitulate, a children's book can be historical, educational, artistic, valuable, decorative, and even a friend. Although expressly designed for children, these unassuming volumes can teach adults a great deal about life's lessons, and perhaps even capture a moment of lost childhood. Care for your acquisitions and they will return benefits tenfold.

Children's books have always made popular gifts, particularly those with illustrations. Taken from an embossed postcard made in Germany, circa 1910.

Bibliography

"Bibliophile in the Nursery," edited by William Targ, The World Publishing Co., Cleveland and New York, 1957.

"Chapbooks of the Eighteenth Century," by John Ashton, Chatto and Windus, Piccadilly, London, 1882.

"The Child and his Book," by Mrs. E.M. Field, 2nd edition, Wells Gardner, Darton & Co., London, 1892. Reissued: Detroit, Singing Tree Press, Book Tower, 1968.

"Children's Books of Yesterday," by Philip James, The Studio Publications Inc., New York, 1933.

"Cobwebs to Catch Flies," Joyce Irene Whalley, University of California Press, Berkeley and Los Angeles, 1975.

"The Collector's Book of Books," by Eric Quayle, Clarkson N. Potter, Inc., Publisher, New York, 1971.

"The Collector's Book of Children's Books," by Eric Quayle, Clarkson N. Potter Pub., New York, 1969.

"A Critical History of Children's Literature," by Meigs, Eaton, Nesbitt, and Viguers, Macmillan Co., London, 1969.

"Early Children's Books and Their Illustration," The Pierpont Morgan Library of New York, text by Gerald Gottlieb, David R. Godine, publisher, Boston, 1975.

"English Children's Books—1600 to 1900," by Percy Muir, Frederick, A. Praeger publisher, New York, 1969.

"How a Book is Made," by Phebe Snow, Routledge and Kegan Paul, London, 1960.

"How to Buy and Sell Old Books," edited by Dr. G.L. Freeman, Century House, The American Life Foundation, Watkins Glen, New York, 1965.

"Illustrated Price Catalog of Old Books Wanted," 4th edition, edited by L.G. Peterson, American Book Mart, Chicago, 1938.

"Kate Greenaway," by Rodney K. Engen, Harmony Books, New York, 1976.

"The Official Guide to Old Books," by William Rodger, House of Collectibles, Florence, Alabama, 1976.

"Old-Time Schools and School-books," by Clifton Johnson, Dover Publications, Inc., New York, 1963.

"One Hundred Nineteenth-Century Rhyming Alphabets in English," from the library of Ruth M. Baldwin, Southern Illinois University Press, Feffer & Simons, Inc., London and Amsterdam, 1972.

"The Osborne Collection of Early Children's Books, 1476–1910," Volume II, prepared by Judith St. John, Toronto Public Library, Toronto, Canada, 1975.

"The Penny Histories," introduction by Victor E. Newburg, Harcourt, Brace & World, Inc., New York, 1969.

"Pictures and Stories from Forgotten Children's Books," Arnold Arnold, Dover Publications, Inc., New York, 1969.

"Powers of Mind," by Adam Smith, Ballantine Books, New York, 1975.

"Processes of Graphic Reproduction in Printing," by Harold Curwen, Faber and Faber, 24 Russell Square, London, 1934.

"Three Centuries of Nursery Rhymes and Poetry for Children," presented by Iona & Peter Opie, Exhibition—The National Book League, Oxford University Press, Ely House, London, 1973.

"The Oxford Dictionary of Nursery Rhymes," edited by Iona and Peter Opie, Oxford at the Clarendon Press, London, 1973.

"When We Were Young," by William Feaver, Holt, Rinehart and Winston, New York, 1977.

Periodicals

"Christie's," South Kensington, 85 Old Brompton Road, London SW 7 3JS, issues from 1975.

"The Bookman Price Index," Daniel F. McGrath, Gale Research Co., Detroit, Michigan, annual issues through 1976.

The author also wishes to thank the "American Collector" magazine for permission to reprint portions of the column, "On Paper" and other articles, as well as "American Antiques" magazine for article reprinting rights.

Index